THE MOVEMENT
OF
WORLD REVOLUTION

Christopher Dawson

SHEED & WARD - NEW YORK

Contents

Grateful acknowledgment is made to the editors of *History Today, Four Quarters, The Commonweal* and the London Times *Literary Supplement* for permission to use here material which first appeared in their pages.

Chapters 6, 9 and 10 were published separately by Sheed and Ward (London) under the title, *The Revolt of Asia*.

Special thanks are owed to Mr. John J. Mulloy for his valuable assistance in the preparation of this volume.

THE MOVEMENT OF
WORLD REVOLUTION

INTRODUCTION

1

The Relevance of European History

WORLD HISTORY, as it is understood today, is an entirely new subject. Sixty years ago, when Acton was planning the Cambridge Modern History, he conceived it as a universal history which would not be a mere combined history of modern states, but a study of the development of universal historical forces. Yet at the same time, he took for granted that this history would be a European one and that it was only, or primarily, in Europe and its colonies that the movement of world history was to be found. But the new conception of World History, as may be seen for example in the UNESCO world history which is being written at the present time, rejects this conception entirely and aspires to produce a work which will be ecumenical in treatment and scope, embracing the whole history of every people from China to Peru without preference or prejudice.

The old European view of history is now condemned as provincial or parochial or "ethnocentric," and it is generally admitted that if we wish to study world history we must pay as much attention to China and India and Islam, not to mention Indonesia and Africa, as to Europe.

At first sight this seems to represent a great advance, but even if this is so, the advance has still to be made. For the great European historians of the past, like Ranke and Acton, were members of an international society of learning and they spoke to a wide audience who knew what they were talking about. Today world history has no such educated public. General historical knowledge has not kept pace with the advance of specialized studies.

And it is inevitable that this should be so, since the linguistic barriers to the study of oriental history are almost insurmountable at the present time, except for a small class of specialists. Thus there is a serious danger that the relative widening of the historical perspective to include the non-European civilizations may be accompanied by an absolute decline in the quality and standard of general European history.

Curiously enough it has been left to an Indian writer—"an unknown Indian," he calls himself, Nirad Chaudhuri—to point out how grave this danger is. He writes as follows:

"In the last few decades there has certainly been seen in Europe, or at all events in England, a decline in historical knowledge, accompanied by a pronounced recoil from the historical attitude. This is a retrograde phenomenon, for if there is anything that distinguishes man from the other animals, it is memory or consciousness of duration, and I cannot understand how the European man, having attained the high degree of historical consciousness that he did in the nineteenth century, can have stepped back from it to the uncultured man's bondage to the present, and the still more uncultured man's bondage to the eschatology of political dogma. Yet what the European man is displaying more often than not today is an utter lack of the historical sense. I sometimes seek the solution of the puzzle in that Spenglerian vision, the dreadful and tragic *Untergang des Abendlandes,* the untimely decline of the European peoples on their home continent, brought about by an internal strife as insensate, as inescapable and as suicidal as that of the Greek cities. I ask myself: Are we witnessing a whole society's senile decay of memory?"[1]

This is a very severe judgment, but it is not altogether lacking in justification. It is borne out for instance by Professor Barraclough's recent volume, *History in a Changing World,* which is all the more instructive because it represents the views of a professional historian as offered to a popular audience. Now Professor Barraclough starts from the conviction that the Russian victory at Stalingrad makes a total revision of European history necessary, and he even goes on not only to discard the nineteenth-century conception of Europe as the centre of universal history, but to question the very existence of Europe as a cultural unity and of any real continuity between classical, medieval and modern history. "The European inheritance," he concludes, "is a tangle of unsolved contradictions, a thicket of dead ends, offering no direct line of advance" for the future. And so instead of the old Western tradition that is centred on Europe and Greece and Rome, he demands a "history that is truly universal—that looks beyond Europe and the West to humanity in all lands and ages." [2]

[1] *The Autobiography of an Unknown Indian* (New York, The Macmillan Company, 1951), p. 341.
[2] The Copp Clark Co., Ltd., Toronto.

Unfortunately, he does not explain how this new history is to be discovered. He does not even suggest where we are to begin. He only refers us to Herr Spengler's view of independent culture cycles and suggests that some new culture is going to arise in Russia or elsewhere—which will in time take the place of the defunct civilization of Europe.

But it would be a mistake to kick away the ladder of European historiography before we have found a foothold in the new world. The fact that Western Europe has lost its position of world leadership does not affect the significance of the European historical tradition. So instead of saying, Farewell to European History, as Alfred Weber and now Professor Barraclough have done, I would rather advocate a Return to European History, since I believe that it is only by way of Europe and the Western historical tradition that it is possible to approach that universal world history which has so long been the ideal of the philosophers of history.

Throughout the past, down to a century or two ago, the historic world was not an intelligible unity. It was made up of a number of independent civilizations, which were like separate worlds, each of them with its own historical tradition and its own idea of world history. During the last thousand years these great world civilizations have been four in number—China, India, Islam and Europe (or rather, Christendom, for the division between Western civilization and its great Eastern neighbours was always a religious rather than a geographical one).

It is true that the isolation of these four cultures was never complete. Europe was in contact with Islam, Islam was in contact with India and India was in contact with China.

But these contacts did not go very deep. In particular they did not extend to a knowledge of the other historical traditions, so that each civilization tended to ignore the historical pasts of the others. Moreover, these four civilizations were far from being world-wide. All together they represented an island of higher civilization in an ocean of darkness. And these barbarous outer lands were seen as lying outside the world of time as well as on the frontiers of the world of space. They were lands without history and even without common humanity.

Now the unique significance of Europe for the development of world history is to be found in the part that it has played in breaking down the isolation of the ancient world civilizations and bringing the unknown outer world into the light of civilization and history. This achievement is so momentous that there is nothing to be compared with it in human history since the original creation of higher civilization (which, however, preceded the dawn of history). Whatever is happening to Europe at the present time or may happen in the future cannot affect the significance of this world-changing event. It must, however, be admitted that modern European historiography has failed to do justice to it. Professor Barraclough is quite right in criticizing the disproportionate amount of attention that has been devoted to the political and diplomatic history of the Western European and North American States—to the English party system, to Frederick the Great and Bismarck and so on—as compared with the all-important question of the relation of Europe to the outer world. Here the nationalist and politicist bias of modern history has distracted attention from the epoch-making changes which have been Europe's real contribution to world history.

It is true that the field is overpoweringly wide and overruns all the conventional limits of conventional academic history. Economics, politics, religion, science and technology are all involved and all exercise a mutual influence on one another. The first step in this process—the breaking of the oceanic barriers of the Old World by the Portuguese and Spanish navigators—is no doubt familiar enough, and yet even here comparatively little study has been devoted to the social and economic background of the movement and to the problem of the continuity between the new forms of colonialism, and those which had already been developed by the Italian maritime republics in their establishments in the Black Sea and the Levant.

The second stage of the European world movement—the penetration of the closed world of the other old-world civilizations—was a much more gradual process, since it began earlier, in the thirteenth century, with the first great travels of the Friars and of Marco Polo to Central Asia, India and China, and has continued throughout the centuries ever since. Here it was the Christian missionaries who played the leading part, though the name of Marco Polo shows that the economic element was also present from the beginning. It was, however, the great missionaries like St. Francis Xavier, Matteo Ricci, Rodolfo Acquaviva, Robert de Nobili and the rest, who alike in India, China and Japan were the first to establish contact between East and West on the higher cultural level. Above all, the Jesuit mission to China in the seventeenth and early eighteenth centuries was unique for its double achievement in convincing Chinese scholars of the scientific values of European culture and in unveiling to Europe the whole extent of Chinese culture—its history, its literature and its institutions. And it is, I think, a legitimate criticism of our current methods of teaching history that for every hundred people who are familiar with the names of the geographical explorers like Tasman and Dampier and Bougainville there is hardly one who knows the names of the scholars who discovered Chinese culture like Ricci, Couplet, de Mailla and du Halde.

The only excuse for this is that the work of the great Jesuit missionaries and scholars belongs to the earlier phase of the European world expansion and did not lead on directly to the triumphant expansion of the third phase. The world hegemony of Western culture was introduced by the three great changes that took place during the eighteenth century—first, the Europeanization of Russia—the one province of Christendom that had remained isolated from the West from the time of the Mongol conquest down to the age of Alexis and Peter the Great; secondly, the establishment of an autonomous centre of Western culture outside Europe in North America; and thirdly, the British conquest of India. Owing to these developments the influence of European culture, which had hitherto been limited to the coasts and the islands, penetrated to the heart of the Asiatic and American continents and gradually subjected the trade and resources of the non-European world to the new Western economic and technical organization.

During the great age of Western capitalism in the nineteenth century, the whole world lay open to the enterprise of the Western financier and merchant and to the skill of the Western technician and engineer. All over the world Europeans and Americans were prospecting for new sources of wealth and opening up new markets and new channels of trade. During its central period, from the time of Adam Smith to that of Cobden and Bright, this economic movement was cosmopolitan rather than imperialist in spirit, and was inspired by the ideals of the liberal Enlightenment. The process which is now regarded as the exploitation of the weaker peoples and classes by Western capitalism was seen by contemporaries as the great means of world progress and international peace. In the words of John Stuart Mill, "It may be said without exaggeration that the great extent and rapid increase of international trade, in being the principal guarantee of the peace of the world, is the great permanent security for the uninterrupted progress of the ideas, the institutions and the character of the human race." In the past, "the patriot wished all countries weak, poor and ill-governed except his own; now he sees in their wealth and progress a direct source of wealth and progress to his own country."[3]

And these ideas were not so absurd as they appear today. So long as the economists and the politicians accepted the Liberal ideology, they were more interested in the expansion of trade than in territorial conquest, and the establishment of a world-wide system of communications was regarded as the common interest of all civilized peoples. As the Roman road was at once the organ and the symbol of the Pax Romana, so the steamship, the railway and the telegraph were the organs of the new pacific world unity which was the ideal of the Western Liberal economists.

[3] *The Principles of Political Economy* (ed. Ashley), 1909, p. 582.

Nor was this expansion of Western culture purely material. It involved the advance of knowledge and the communication of ideas—and that in both directions. Towards
the end of the eighteenth century, Western science took up
the work of the Jesuit missionaries and began to reveal an
unknown world of oriental religion and philosophy. The
discovery of Sanskrit literature (by Anquetil-Duperron, Sir
William Jones, Sir Charles Wilkins and Henry Colebrooke)
was one of the most epoch-making events of modern times.
In the West, it prepared the way for an oriental renaissance
which had a profound effect on European thought, especially in Germany and France, in the first decades of the
nineteenth century. At the same time, in the East, the influence of Western ideas, combined with the European interest
in Sanskrit studies, produced important changes in Indian
culture. The spread of education, the development of the
vernacular literatures, above all Bengali, and the influence
of personalities like Ram Mohun Roy (1780–1833) and
Debindra Nath Tagore prepared the way for the revival of
Hindu culture and the growth of a new educated class and
a new national spirit. Thus it was the West that created Indian nationalism by giving India a new sense of its cultural
values and achievements.

This two-sided process of Western scientific study and
oriental cultural awakening went on all over the East during
the nineteenth century and has extended in the present century to the more primitive peoples of Africa and the Pacific.
Here Europe achieved something that had never been done
before, since neither the Greeks nor the Arabs nor the Per-
sians, in spite of their interest in the manners and customs
of strange peoples, ever succeeded in getting inside the

minds of the societies that they studied and comprehending their culture as a living whole. Today this has become the normal procedure of the modern social anthropologist, but its origins are much older than scientific anthropology, and are to be found in the new oriental and historical studies. Edward Lane's *Account of the Manners and Customs of the Modern Egyptians,* published in 1836, is a classical type of what I mean, though no doubt it is by no means the earliest example. It seems to me to be closely related to the achievements of nineteenth-century historians—to works like de Tocqueville's work on American democracy, on the one hand, and to Fustel de Coulanges' book on the Ancient City or Burckhardt's study of the Renaissance, on the other.

No doubt this new historical and sociological humanism was the work of a small elite. For one man like Lane or Mountstuart Elphinstone or Brian Hodgson, there were a hundred Jos Sedleys or William Hickeys, and if there had been more of the former type, the history of the modern world would have been very different.

But, on the other hand, it may be argued that it was Kipling's "Sons of Martha," the engineers and civil servants and sanitary inspectors, who performed the essential task of breaking through the inherited tyranny of prejudice and custom and thrusting the new scientific and technical order on a hundred unwilling peoples. It may be objected that this function might have been performed by the oriental peoples themselves without Western control. But Japan is the only example of a people accepting a radical change in its way of life without being forced to do so by Western economic or political power. The natural reaction of oriental nationalism to Western contact was reactionary in both senses of the word. Those reactionary nationalists or traditionalists who led the resistance to Western imperialism in the nineteenth century were by no means inferior in character to the leaders of the later nationalist movements—some of them, like 'Abd al Khadir in Algeria, Shamyl in the Caucasus, the Khalifa 'Abdullah in the Egyptian Sudan, were heroic figures, but they were doomed to inevitable defeat because they did not possess the techniques and the scientific organization of the civilization that they resisted. All the triumphs of modern oriental nationalism have been the work of men of Western education, who were able to use the ideas and knowledge of the West in the service of their own peoples.

This new class was, however, literary rather than scientific in training. It was composed, especially in India and in the Near East, of lawyers and journalists and schoolmasters, rather than engineers and doctors and economists. It remained for a long time suspended between two worlds—filled with enthusiasm for the material civilization and democratic ideals of the West, but still profoundly attached to the memory of its ancient cultural traditions.

Hence the ambivalence of the modern nationalist movements. The Westernized intelligentsia acted as the spearhead of national mass movements which were animated by anti-Western xenophobia. But the moment that independence had been secured, they took over the role of the European administrators and proceeded to modernize oriental society far more drastically than the old colonialism had ever dared to do. And this tendency is most pronounced in Communist states, where the traditional religious foundations of oriental

culture are being destroyed just as ruthlessly as the alien
power of Western capitalism, which is much less deeply
rooted. Thus the movement of world change that was inaugurated in Western Europe several centuries ago has now
been so fully assimilated by the East that it is being carried
forward by the very forces that are most overtly hostile to
the West. And though this may well mean the end of the
political predominance of Europe, it certainly cannot be
used as an argument against the significance of the Western
achievement. It is in fact a process which was foreseen and
foretold by some of the typical representatives of nineteenth-
century—and perhaps eighteenth-century—Liberalism, for
their idealism was cosmopolitan rather than nationalist in
its outlook. As Walt Whitman, the most aggressive booster
of the West, proclaimed, the great adventure of Western
Man, the discovery of the New World, is at the same time
a passage to India and more than India; the voyage of the
mind's return to its first wisdom—the understanding of the
past and the comprehension of the whole, and the meeting
of the two opposite poles of the globe in a united humanity.

This liberal idealism seems very remote from the racial
and cultural conflicts of the existing situation, not only in
Europe, but in Asia, Africa and the Middle East. Nevertheless we are witnessing far-reaching attempts to establish relations between Eastern and Western culture and to create
an organized system of world order, and both of these movements are the direct products of nineteenth-century Western
ideas. No doubt it is only too easy to conceive the break-
down of these attempts and the return by way of oriental
and African nationalism to a system of closed cultures. But

this offers no real prospect of a new creative culture cycle. Rather it suggests the coming of a new dark age and the gradual decline of the standards of culture. The only real alternative to the tradition of Western Liberalism is that of Eastern Communism, and this is so deeply committed to the principles of Western science and technology and to one version of Western social and political ideas that it can hardly be regarded as representative of oriental culture.

But neither can it be regarded as completely Western. It seems a kind of *tertium quid:* an intermediate power which stands in a somewhat similar position to the European state and to Western socialism as the reformed Tsardom of Peter the Great did to the Enlightened Monarchy of Europe in the eighteenth century. But in spite of the distance that Russian and oriental Communism has travelled from its Marxian origins in practice, it still remains completely faithful to the Marxian theory, and most of all in its theory of history. The Communist philosophy of history is still the original theory which Marx derived from his study of French politics, English economics and Hegelian metaphysics. And in spite of all the attempts that have been made to adjust this theory to non-European realities, the system still retains clear marks of its Western origin, being fully intelligible only when it is seen in its original nineteenth-century Western European setting.

No doubt it is possible to explain the development of Communism in different and non-Western terms. It might be seen as a reversion to the social and political traditions of the oriental state. After all, in Marx's own youth a very remarkable experiment in state capitalism was being carried out in the Near East which in many respects foreshadows the recent developments of state planning in Communist countries. In the first half of the nineteenth century Mehemet Ali was carrying out a revolutionary reorganization of the Egyptian national economy. The landlords were expropriated, a new system of irrigation was introduced and the peasants were compelled to cultivate new crops for the export market. At the same time new industries were created and state factories established. By 1830 it is said that ninety-five per cent of the total exports and forty per cent of the imports were on behalf of the state.

It is easy to see a parallel between this bold attempt to collectivize and industrialize a peasant economy by direct bureaucratic control, and what Stalin did in Russia under his successive five-year plans; even the details are similar—the resistance of the Kulaks, the sabotage of the new machines, the shortage of consumer goods and the sacrifice of the peasants' standard of living to the requirements of the state trading system. Certainly neither system has much in common with the Marxian ideal of the workers' state, even under the dictatorship of the proletariat.

But however true this may be, it is not recognized by the Communists themselves. They are bound to remain faithful in theory to the Western aspect of Communism, because it is this element which gives the movement its popular appeal. For if Communism were seen as a return to the oriental tradition of state autocracy, if Stalin were regarded as a Russian Mehemet Ali, it would no longer evoke the hopes of the masses, since it would represent the cause of the oppressor rather than the cause of the oppressed. The elements in Marxism which are derived from the common tradition of

Western socialism and democracy—the appeal to justice, humanity and the rights of man, even though they are not realized in the totalitarian practice of the Communist state, are still absolutely essential to the success of Communist propaganda in the East no less than in the West; and thus Communism remains committed to Western social ideals.

So too with oriental nationalism. This also owes its moral appeal and its positive qualities to the political ideals it has acquired from the West. Modern nationalism is an exotic growth in Asia and Africa and its diffusion has followed closely on the spread of Western education. If it loses this leaven of Western ideals and becomes a negative xenophobic reaction against the West, it also becomes a destructive force. We saw this in India at the time of partition when the old mass loyalties asserted themselves in their naked elemental violence and the educated leaders of Indian nationalism recoiled in horror. But perhaps the most striking example of the strength of the Western element in oriental nationalism is the case of modern Turkey, where the Kemalist revival which arose in the hour of defeat to save the Turkish nation from external conquest ended by transforming Turkey into a modern secular state planned on strictly Western lines.

Thus it seems to me impossible to avoid the conclusion that the new Asia and Africa which are emerging with such revolutionary suddenness do not represent simply the reaction of Asiatic or African culture against the influence of an alien civilization, but rather the extension of Western civilization and Western international society into the extra-European world.

It is a process which may be compared with the move-

ment of national liberation in the Balkans during the nineteenth century, vastly different though it is in scale and
results. For the liberation of the Balkans did not mean a
return to the cultural traditions of their Byzantine past; it
meant the opening of the Balkans to Western civilization
and the gradual incorporation of the liberated nations into
the society of European peoples. It may be objected in the
case of Asia that this expansion of Western civilization was
the work of colonialism and that the destruction of colonialism is the *raison d'être* of oriental nationalism. Certainly
colonialism was the first stage of the process. As Karl Marx
wrote more than a century ago, in an article on India in
the *New York Times* of August 8th, 1853, England had to
annihilate the old Asiatic society before it was possible to
lay the material foundations of Western society in Asia. But
when once this function had been performed, colonialism
exercised a restrictive influence by protecting the institutions and interests which were rooted in the old order, as
we see in the case of the Indian Princes and client states.
The new order in Asia is the work of the new classes that
were created by Western education and Western economy,
and they have more in common with their opposite numbers
in Europe and America—professors and journalists and
industrialists and politicians—than with the priests and
princes and peasants who were the authentic representatives
of the tradition of Asiatic culture.

Alike in the Communist and non-Communist countries,
the chief problems that confront the new societies are educational and technological. They have to carry out with
great rapidity and on an enormous scale the changes which

were introduced slowly, step by step, in Europe and America in the course of centuries. Although they are all of them very conscious of the great traditions of oriental culture, they cannot look to these traditions for guidance in the work they have to do. Even in education, where the achievements of the ancient cultures were most remarkable, the break with the past has been almost complete. In India, Western education was firmly established long before the coming of independence, and though there has naturally been a reaction against the extreme occidentalism of nineteenth-century education, there has been no question of a return to Brahmin tradition. In China, on the other hand, the great tradition of Confucian education was still dominant in the nineteenth century, but it was the most formidable obstacle to the new ideas and therefore has been treated by the reformers as a reactionary force.

Thus alike in education, in technology and in economic policy, the peoples of Asia look to the modern West rather than to the ancient East for practical economic assistance and for theoretical, scientific and political principles: while at the same time their nationalism is based on an anti-colonial and anti-Western ideology which makes them intensely suspicious of Western political influence. And these two contradictory tendencies are the real explanation of the advance of Communism in Asia. Communism appeals to the peoples of Asia because it offers the alternative of a modern scientific technological order which is distinct from and opposed to the West as they have known it—to the old English and Dutch colonialism and to the new American business empire. Hence the non-Communist states are seriously handicapped, since their nationalist ideology makes it difficult for them to co-operate with the West as wholeheartedly as China can co-operate with the U.S.S.R., in spite of the fact that the latter demands much more drastic changes in the Asiatic way of life and in its religious traditions and institutions. But whichever party triumphs, the invasion of the East and of Africa by Western ideologies and technology goes on without ceasing and the institutions and traditions of the ancient cultures continue to decline.

It seems as though the whole world, East and West, were moving by two different roads towards the same goal—towards a common world civilization, based on science, technology, social democracy and popular education.

But these two roads are very far apart from one another: on the one hand the divided, many-branched ways of democratic nationalism, and on the other the straight, hard, bloody highroad of Communist revolution; so that instead of conducting the nations to a common goal, they seem to be leading them apart to the destruction of civilization by the intensification of ideological and communal conflict.

In this total world situation, Western Europe can no longer hope to play a dominant political role, either for good or evil, but Western civilization in its modern extension to America and Russia still remains the heart of the conflict and the centre of modern world history.

And if we wish to understand the roots of the conflict and the source of the revolutionary movements of change that are transforming and possibly destroying the world, it is to Europe in the traditional sense that we must look. As the new science and technology are European in origin, so also is it with the political and ideological conflicts of the present age. These conflicts were in their origin European ones, going back to the age of the French Revolution and to the party conflicts that divided Western socialists and liberal nationalists in the nineteenth century—to the days when Marx and Mazzini, Bakunin and Louis Blanc, Kossuth and Herzen all lived together in exile and waged their little ideological wars in London lodging houses. But today these conflicts are being fought out by Asiatic mass societies which know nothing of this cosy nineteenth-century background— societies which are neither bourgeois nor proletarian, and whose idea of nationality is founded on vast civilizations comparable to Europe or Christendom rather than to historic political unities like the Western European nations.

Nevertheless, the study of the European past is still relevant to modern world history, since Europe was the original source of the movement of change in which the whole world is now involved and it is in European history that we find the key to the understanding of the ideologies which divide the modern world. Indeed it must be admitted that historians themselves have a heavy share in the responsibility for the creation of these ideologies. No doubt it may be said that ideological history such as we find in Stalin's *Short History of the Communist Party,* or Rosenberg's *Myth of the Twentieth Century* is a grotesque caricature of true history. Nevertheless, such perversions would have been impossible if there had not been something seriously wrong with European history in the second half of the nineteenth century.

Modern nationalism would never have become so formidable if it had not been inflated by the genius of the great

THE REVOLUTION IN
WESTERN CULTURE

2

Renaissance and Reformation

THE period of modern history which extends from the Reformation to the French Revolution is a very difficult one to study and, I believe, there is a real danger that it may become increasingly neglected, especially by Catholic scholars. In the past and, indeed, until quite recently this period was regarded as "Modern History" and it was the main object of study not only by the popular literary historians, like Macaulay and Carlyle and Froude, but no less by the great men of learning, like Ranke and Acton, whose vast knowledge and powers of research have never been surpassed. But today Modern History has acquired a new meaning. More and more historians are devoting themselves to the study of the immediate past. New fields of study are being brought into the domain of history, while the wars and revolutions through which the world has passed in the present generation have changed our perspective and have made the Europe of the seventeenth century as remote as—and to Catholics, perhaps, more remote than—that of the thirteenth century. These centuries no longer belong to Modern History. Although they are not medieval in the technical sense, they are as it were a new middle age which separates modern Europe from medieval Christendom.

Nevertheless, though this period no longer belongs to "modern history," it still retains its importance since it is the age out of which modern Europe and the modern world have come. It is the age that saw the creation of the national state, the creation of modern science and the flowering of the modern vernacular literatures. Above all it is the age which saw the expansion of Western culture from its original West European centre to America and to the world. And it has a peculiar and tragic interest for Christians, because it was the age which saw the division of Christendom, when the Catholic and Protestant worlds assumed their existing forms and when Western culture began to undergo that process of secularization which has only been completed in our own days. If we do not understand this age, we cannot be said to understand European culture at all or American culture either.

Yet it is a very difficult age for us to understand; in some ways even more difficult than the Middle Ages proper. In the first place, we have always been taught to approach it from a strictly national standpoint. And though it is easy enough to study the England of the Tudors or the France of Louis XIV from this national angle, this makes it all the more difficult to study Europe as a whole. For then, as always, the typical European movements crossed the national frontiers and set up complex international relations which changed the national part as well as the European whole. The Renaissance, the Reformation, the Catholic Revival, the Enlightenment were all international movements, though each of them owed much to the leadership of some particular people. For while it is natural and right that we should study political history in terms of states or political units, it is also right that we should study civilization in terms of cultures.

In spite of the doubts of the positivist, a culture is just as much a sociological reality as a state. Indeed it is more real inasmuch as it has a larger social content. For it is at once a common way of life based on a common social tradition and also a spiritual community based on common beliefs and ideas. But while this conception of culture has become fundamental in the work of the modern anthropologist and pre-historian, it is still comparatively unfamiliar to the historian of modern Europe. And it is mainly on this account that the period of which I am speaking is so difficult to study, since, in spite of the immense wealth and variety of historical literature, there is a remarkable lack of standard works on European culture as a whole, especially during the seventeenth century when the Baroque culture of Catholic Europe transcended national and political frontiers as the culture of medieval Christendom had done.

This is particularly unfortunate because the age of which I am speaking began with two great international movements—the Renaissance and the Reformation—which had a profound effect on European culture and which cannot be explained in political or national terms. Neither can they be explained in terms of one another. In spite of the intimate and complex relations between them, both alike are aspects of the great cultural revolution which was due to the dis-

solution of the medieval unity of Western Christendom and
to the reorganization of the different elements of Western
culture according to new patterns. Throughout the medieval
centuries from Charlemagne to the Council of Constance
the unity of Western Christendom had been the basis of
Western European culture. No doubt it is easy to exaggerate
and to idealize this unity, but when everything has been said
the fact remains that the Catholic Church was the mould in
which all the diverse social elements of the Western society
were brought together and fused into cultural unity. It gave
the peoples of the West not only a common faith, but a
common intellectual education, a common moral law, and
a common system of organization. Technically the organization was an ecclesiastical one, but it entered into every
aspect of social life and was in many ways stronger and
more effective than the nascent political organization of the
European state. For it was the Pope and not the Emperor
who was the true head of Christendom, and he exercised a
real superpolitical authority over the Kings and Princes of
Western Europe.

Nevertheless, this Papal supremacy did not involve an
Italian hegemony. The centre of the common culture lay
north of the Alps in the area between the Rhine, the Rhone,
and the Loire, and it was in this centre that the creative
movements of medieval culture had their origin. In the
eighth and ninth centuries it was the centre of the Carolingian empire and the Carolingian culture. In the tenth and
eleventh centuries it was the source of the movement of
monastic and ecclesiastical reform which had its centre in
Lorraine and Burgundy, and it was the alliance of these two

movements with the Papacy which determined the form of medieval Christendom and the character of its culture. So, too, in the following period this area was the source of the Crusading movement and of the Cistercian reform, and the centre of the university movement, of the scholastic philosophy and of Gothic architecture and art.

But the later Middle Ages saw the decline of all these movements except the last. Monasticism decayed, the Crusade was abandoned, the scholastic synthesis disintegrated under the influence of Nominalism, and the alliance between the Papacy and the movement of ecclesiastical reform was dissolved. And at the same time the focal area of medieval culture was divided and ruined by the destructive conflict of the Hundred Years War and the internecine feud between France and Burgundy. The Council of Constance represented a final effort of medieval Christendom to recover its lost unity. Thenceforth, the axis of Western culture shifted to the south.

In the Italian cities during the later Middle Ages, a new kind of society was being formed which differed radically from the feudal society of Northern Europe and tended to reproduce the old patterns of Mediterranean city culture. As the Northern culture centre declined, this revived Mediterranean culture grew in strength and self-confidence and became increasingly conscious of the great traditions of the past. This consciousness was increased by the fact that the Italian cities were now the dominant power in the Eastern Mediterranean and were thus brought into contact with a civilization older and more refined than that of continental Europe. For although the Byzantine Empire was moribund,

Byzantine culture was still a living force, and the beginning of the fifteenth century was even marked by a certain cultural revival inspired by Hellenic as distinct from Byzantine traditions. The centres of this revival were in European Greece, at Mistra in the Peloponnese, and at Athens, which was at that time the capital of a Florentine dynasty and the meeting place of Byzantine and Italian influences. Thus at the time of the Council of Florence (1439) the two movements of Italian and Greek culture were able to meet on equal terms, and the advent of Byzantine scholars, like Manuel Chrysoloras, Gemisthos Plethon, Demetrius Chalcondyles, Theodore Gaza, and Cardinal Bessarion stimulated the revival of Greek culture in Italy. Although nineteenth-century historians often interpret this movement as neo-pagan and hostile to the traditions of Christian culture, it was in fact regarded with favour by the Church, and its leaders throughout the Renaissance period held key positions in the Papal court and chancery. Indeed the alliance of the Papacy and the humanists was one of the dominant features of fifteenth-century culture and replaced the alliance between the Papacy and the monastic reformers which was characteristic of the eleventh and twelfth centuries.

Meanwhile in Northern Europe the preoccupation with the reform of the Church still persisted. But it was no longer associated with monasticism or with the Papacy. It tended rather to express itself in heretical or schismatic movements and to ally itself with the rising forces of nationalism and the national state as we see in the Hussite movement and even in that of Wycliffe which preceded it. Even the more orthodox reforming movement which expressed itself at the councils of Constance and Basel became increasingly hostile to the Papacy, so that at the very moment when Pope Eugenius IV and the Byzantine Emperor and patriarch had succeeded in ending the ancient schism between East and West, the West as represented by the Council of Basel was deposing the Pope and asserting the supremacy of the General Council against the Papacy.

It is true that the schism of Basel soon came to an inglorious end, but the neutrality manifested by Germany and so many of the northern princes showed how doubtful the allegiance of the West to the unity of Christendom had become. During the next seventy years the importance of the question of the reform of the Church was universally recognized, but no effective action was taken. The Papacy became increasingly absorbed in Italian politics while the northern rulers used the demand for reform as an excuse for extending their control over the Church in their dominions. Nor should we assume that the interest in reform was confined to the conciliar party or to Northern Europe. The Italians and even the humanists themselves were fully conscious of the need for reform. The greatest of the humanists, Pope Pius II, was also one of the last champions of the unity of medieval Christendom and the medieval idea of the Crusade, though at the same time he was well aware of the decline of these ideals and of the way in which national rivalries and political ambitions were destroying the unity of Christian society.

The European situation was ripe for an explosion. Martin Luther was simply the revolutionary leader whose passionate genius fired the train. He was the living embodiment of all the elements in Northern Europe which were most alien from Rome and from the new Mediterranean culture. He appealed from Hellenism to Hebraism, from Italian humanism to Northern religious emotion, from the authority of the Roman Papacy to the Christian Nobility of the German Nation. There was, however, one respect in which he agreed with the humanists: he shared their distaste for asceticism. The circumstances of his conversion caused him to react with extraordinary violence against the monastic life and the ascetic ideal on which it was founded, above all the ideal of virginity. And this was one of the most revolutionary aspects of his work, for the monks had been the makers of Western Christendom. They had dominated medieval culture from its beginnings down to the thirteenth century when their influence had been replaced by that of the friars, who represented the same ascetic ideal in a more popular and personal form.

Moreover monasticism was not peculiar to Western Christendom. It was common to the whole Christian world from Russia to Abyssinia, and to the whole Christian past since the fourth century, so that its destruction changed not only the social and institutional pattern of medieval culture but also the moral and spiritual ideals of the Christian life. Religion was secularized in the sense that it was reorientated from the cloister to the world and found its centre in the family and in the active fulfillment of man's earthly calling. No doubt all this was secondary in Luther's eyes to the fundamental evangelical doctrine of salvation by faith alone. But the destructive element of the Protestant revolution was more far-reaching than the positive, and was to some extent independent of it, as we see in the early history of the English Reformation.

For Henry VIII had no sympathy or understanding for Luther's religious ideas. The tradition to which he appealed was that of Philip le Bel and Louis of Bavaria, as we see from his publication of works like Marsilius' *Defensor Pacis* and the *dialogus inter Militem et Clericum* of which English translations were produced in 1533 and 1535. And so long as his schism followed these conservative lines it met with little resistance from clergy or people. But when from political and economic motives he followed the Protestant example and attacked the monasteries, the revolutionary character of his work became clear and it aroused a wave of popular Catholic feeling which under more vigorous leadership might have changed the course of history.

The Reformation was a revolutionary movement not merely on account of the excesses of fanatical minorities, like the Zwickau prophets or the Anabaptists of Münster, but because it changed both the spiritual and social order of the medieval world. Nothing is more remarkable than the rapidity with which the movement spread across the whole of northern Europe in the course of a few years from Switzerland to the Rhine to Scandinavia and the remote territories of Livonia and Courland. In these years the resistance of the Catholics was insignificant. The religious orders, notably the Augustinian Friars, were themselves the leaders of the revolt and before the Catholic forces had had time to rally, Germany had become three quarters Protestant and Scandinavia and the Baltic lands almost completely so. Only Iceland stood out for a little. When the first Icelandic monastery was destroyed by the Danes in 1539, the perpetrators were outlawed by the Althing and the governor was deposed. It was not until 1550 that the last Catholic bishop Jan Arason, the poet, was executed at Skalholt with his two sons.

But while it is impossible to exaggerate the importance of Luther as the source of the revolutionary movement which destroyed the unity of Christendom and split Europe asunder, his achievements as a constructor and organizer were relatively small and it is very doubtful whether Lutheranism would have withstood the Catholic reaction that followed if it had been left to its own resources. The wider development of Protestantism as a European movement which met the Catholic Counter Reformation on its own ground was mainly due to a genius of a very different type.

John Calvin was a French bourgeois, the son of a lawyer at Noyon, who brought to the service of the Protestant cause the logic and discipline and legal acuteness of the Latin mind. Unlike Luther he was essentially an intellectual, a scholar and a man of letters. But he was an intellectual who had the gift of ruling men, and from his study he was able at once to govern a state and to direct a world-wide movement of religious propaganda and ecclesiastical organization. In place of the somewhat shapeless and incoherent mass of doctrines and tendencies represented by Luther and the German reformers, he fashioned a coherent logical body of doctrine and an iron system of discipline, and in place of the state-controlled Lutheran territorial Churches, he created an autonomous Church which claimed theocratic authority. In this respect Calvinism inherited the tradition of the Catholic reforming movement of the Middle Ages, since it maintained the supremacy of the spiritual power as uncompromisingly as St. Gregory VII had done and was equally ready to resist any attempt on the part of the state to interfere in the government of the Church.

Thus in spite of the theological principles that were common to Lutheranism and Calvinism, their social appeal and their political effects were entirely different. Lutheranism had appealed to the princes and had transferred to the state the prerogatives and power and property which had belonged to the Church. Calvinism, on the other hand, appealed to the people, and especially to the newly educated middle classes, to which Calvin himself belonged. In the same way, while in Germany Protestantism soon lost the support of the humanists, so that Luther found his most formidable opponent in Erasmus, the leader of the intelligentsia, in France it was in humanist circles that the success of Calvinism was most pronounced, so that the leaders of Cisalpine humanism in the later sixteenth century, like J. J. Scaliger and Isaac Casaubon, were found among the Calvinists. In this way the Reformation in its second phase did a good deal to promote the cause of learning. The Calvinists, no less than their enemies, the Jesuits, fully realized the importance of education, and wherever they went, even as far as Massachusetts Bay, they brought not only the Bible but also the Latin Grammar.

Nevertheless this humanism was of a strictly utilitarian kind. Its adherents were the friends of education, but they were the enemies of culture and did their best to destroy and dissipate the wealth of religious art and imagery which had been accumulated by centuries of Christian culture. It was this fierce spirit of iconoclasm and the harsh intolerance that the Calvinists showed towards all the manifestations of Catholic piety which made any reconciliation between Protestantism and the movement of Catholic reform impossible and doomed Europe to more than a century of religious war and sectarian controversy.

The reaction to the tremendous changes brought about by Luther and Calvin also spread to the Mediterranean world. When Luther launched his revolt, the culture of humanist Italy had reached its maturity and Leo X, the son of Lorenzo de Medici, had made Rome the centre of a brilliant literary and artistic culture. Centuries later men looked back on the Rome of Leo X as a golden age. Voltaire writes of it as one of those rare moments in the history of the world which vindicate the greatness of the human mind and compensate the historian for the barren prospect of a thousand years of stupidity and barbarism. To Luther, on the other hand, the Rome of Leo X was a sink of iniquity, its culture was pure materialism, and its religion was gross superstition.

Neither of these extremes is justified. Leo X's generous patronage of culture cannot redeem his failures in his spiritual and international leadership. And the worldliness and moral laxity of Italian society do not prove that Italian religion was moribund. On the contrary its vitality is shown by the unbroken series of saints and mystics and reformers who flourished throughout the Renaissance period and who are to be found not only among the representatives of the medieval tradition like Savonarola but among the leaders of humanist culture. At Rome itself in the age of Leo X, the Oratory of Divine Love, out of which the Theatine Order arose a few years later, formed a centre of spiritual renewal which united leaders of the Catholic reform like St. Cajetan and Cardinal Carafa (afterwards Paul IV) with humanists and members of the Papal court, like Sadolet and Manetti, and later Reginald Pole, Aleander and Contarini.

The spirit of this Italian reforming movement was at once more medieval and more modern than that of the German Reformation. It aimed at applying the interior spirituality of the Italian mystical tradition—the spirit of St. Catherine of Genoa—to the task of ecclesiastical reform, and instead of revolting against the monastic and the ascetic traditions like Luther, it sought to adapt them to the needs of the age by providing a corporate quasi-monastic way of life in which the clergy could carry on their pastoral work, while living by rule in community. This innovation proved extraordinarily popular and successful. It exerted its influence not only by training priests and bishops but even more by providing an example which was to be followed by a series of similar institutions, the Barnabites of St. Antonio Maria Zaccaria, the Somaschi of St. Jerome Emiliani, above all the Roman Oratory of St. Philip Neri. It was this movement, even more than the Spanish Counter Reformation, which was the real source of the Catholic revival and of the new forms and ideals of modern Catholicism.

Nevertheless it did not possess the dynamic quality that was necessary to meet the challenge of the Reformation. The Christian humanists might have reason and authority and tradition on their side, but they were too civilized to cope

with the titanic forces which had been released by Martin
Luther.

But the Mediterranean world also possessed a new source
of spiritual energy which was still intact. The rising force
of nationality was making itself felt in the Iberian Peninsula
no less than in Germany, but in Spain, unlike Germany, it
was directed and unified by a strong central power. After
centuries of division and strife the Spanish Kingdoms had
been united in 1474 by the Catholic Kings who set themselves to reorganize and reform the whole national order,
alike in Church and State. In this task they were able to
appeal to the age-long tradition of the crusade against the
infidel which had always been the dynamic force in Spanish
history, so that they could unite their peoples externally by
the reconquest of the remaining Moslem territories in Southern Spain and internally by the liquidation of the non-
Christian minorities through the tribunal of the Inquisition,
which was the organ of national unity as well as of Catholic
orthodoxy and helped to identify the spirit of Spanish patriotism with Spanish religious ideals.

Hence the conquest of Granada in 1492, instead of mark-
ing the end of the Spanish crusade, only strengthened their
sense of a national mission and transferred their crusading
energy to new fields. At the same moment Spain became a
great imperial power, owing first to the discovery of America, secondly to the conquest of Naples and finally to the
union with Burgundy and Austria, which brought Spain into
association with the Empire and hence into collision with
the German Reformation. While the Flemish advisers of
Charles V followed a policy of moderation and were not

unsympathetic to Erasmus' conciliatory ideas, the Spaniards saw the religious conflict as the opportunity for a new crusade. As early as the Spring of 1521, the Council of Castille wrote to the Emperor, reminding him of the sacrifices which the Catholic Kings had made for the faith and begging him to call "the warlike and Christian Germans" to arms in order to seize Luther and send him a prisoner to Rome for the judgment of the Holy Father.

It was this Spanish crusading spirit which was to become the motive force of the Counter Reformation. By degrees it communicated itself to Charles V and his advisers so that eventually, and still more under his successor, the whole resources of the Spanish Empire were mobilized in a new holy war against European Protestantism.

Nevertheless this militant aggressiveness was only one aspect of Spanish Catholicism. Still more important was its internal spiritual mission for the reform of the Church and the restoration of Catholic culture, which found its expression in the work of St. Ignatius Loyola and the Society of Jesus. The beginnings of Ignatius were those of a spiritual Quixote, a knight errant in search of a crusade. But his retreat at Manresa, which coincided with that of Luther at the Wartburg, transformed his character and his aims and revealed to him his true mission, which was both internal and universal. The society which he created united the spirit of the Spanish Counter Reformation with that of the Italian movement of spiritual reform which was represented by the Theatines and later by the Oratory. Unlike the former it was essentially international in character and was directly dependent on the Papacy, but it also embodied the Spanish crusading ideal in a sublimated form, as we see above all in the heroic achievements of St. Francis Xavier, the apostle of the Indies.

No less important, however, in the long run was the activity of the Society of Jesus in education and culture. From the sixteenth century onwards the Jesuits set themselves to adapt the new methods of humanist education to Christian ideals, and their colleges, which were established all over the Catholic world from Peru to Russia, were the organs of a common type of humanist Catholic culture. Their work did more than anything else to restore the prestige of Catholic education, which had been so much damaged by the assaults of the humanists against the old scholastic tradition. And at the same time the work of the Jesuits as directors of conscience and spiritual advisers brought the influence of the Catholic revival to bear on the courts and cabinets, which were the key points of social influence and had hitherto been the centre of the disintegrating movements that had undermined the unity of Christendom.

But great as the contribution of the Society to the Catholic revival was, it was only a part of a much wider development. For example, the revival of the contemplative life and the new flowering of Christian mysticism, which was the spiritual climax of the whole movement, owed less to the Jesuits than to the Carmelite Reform, which arose slightly later and did not attain its full influence on the Catholic world until the early years of the seventeenth century. St. Teresa and St. John of the Cross, no less than St. Ignatius and St. Francis Xavier, are a proof of the extraordinary dynamism of the Spanish religious genius, and their achieve-

ment is even more representative of the Spanish religious
tradition than that of the great Jesuits, since it is the culmination of a mystical tradition that was already flourishing,
especially among the Spanish Franciscans, like Francisco
of Ossuna, Bernardino of Laredo and St. Peter of Alcan-
tara. Nevertheless it would be a mistake to ascribe the mystical revival of the sixteenth century entirely to Spanish
sources. It had its independent roots in Italy, where one of
the greatest of Catholic mystics, St. Catherine of Genoa
(1447–1497), had had a profound influence on the spiritual life of Renaissance Italy through Christian humanists
like Ettore Vernazza.

It is difficult to overestimate the share of the mystics in
the Catholic revival and their influence on the new Catholic
culture. The Protestant criticisms of Catholicism as a religion of external practices lost all their force when they were
confronted with this new outpouring of divine grace and
with the ideal of spiritual perfection manifested in the lives
of the saints. At the same time mysticism provided the anti-
dote against the rationalist and materialist tendencies in
Western society and enlarged the range of humanist culture
by a deeper and more sublime vision of spiritual reality,
which inspired poets and artists as well as theologians and
philosophers.

This too is an important factor in the Catholic revival,
for the centres of the Catholic renaissance were also the
centres of artistic production, so that Catholic art became
one of the great channels for the diffusion of Catholic culture. Thus it is that the new Baroque art has given its name
to the new culture which became the last great corporate

expression of Western religious ideals. For the expansion of the Baroque culture was not merely an ideological movement, like the Enlightenment in the eighteenth century or the diffusion of nineteenth-century Liberalism. It appealed to the heart as well as the head and satisfied the emotional as well as the intellectual needs of human nature. And thus it was never merely the culture of an educated minority, since its religious ideals embodied in painting and architecture and music were the common heritage of the people as a whole and not the exclusive possession of a privileged class.

Owing to this character, the Baroque culture possessed exceptional powers of diffusion even among peoples of alien traditions. On the whole, the modern expansion of European culture has been external and material. It has forced non-European peoples to recognize the superiority of Western techniques and Western scientific knowledge, but it has failed to bridge the spiritual gap between East and West. But within the sphere of the Baroque culture this was not so. Mexico and Peru and the Portuguese settlements in Asia assimilated the Baroque culture and produced their own local styles of Baroque art.

Thus by the seventeenth century Europe and the new world were sharply divided between two apparently exclusive and antagonistic forms of culture. The Inquisition and the ecclesiastical control of books and ideas, on the one hand, and the penal laws against Catholicism, on the other, seemed to create an impassable barrier which divided Catholic and Protestant Europe and America into two closed worlds. How was it, under these circumstances, that the unity of Western culture survived? Why did not the Baroque culture of Catholic Europe and the Protestant culture of the North go their own ways and gradually diverge further and further from one another until they became as mutually incomprehensible and as spiritually remote as Christendom and Islam?

The reason for this is to be found not so much in their common Christianity but in their common humanism. Both Catholic and Protestant Europe shared the same humanist education and the same classical literature, so that in spite of their spiritual separation they still maintained a certain community of intellectual life which prevented the divergence between Catholics and Protestants from completely destroying the unity of Western culture.

I do not go so far as to say that the humanist culture of the post-Reformation world was one and the same in every part of Europe. Religious differences had an even greater influence than national ones on its development, so that while Catholics and Protestants were alike influenced by their humanist education, it yielded different products in art and thought and life in different spiritual environments. Thus while humanism had as strong an influence on education and literature in Protestant Europe as in Catholic Europe it permeated the whole culture less deeply than it did the Baroque culture of the South. It produced great scholars like Scaliger and Casaubon and great poets like Milton, but it remained the culture of a minority. The educated classes had all undergone the discipline of humane letters, but the people as a whole derived their moral ideas and their spiritual imagery not from the philosophers or the humanists or the artists but directly from the Bible and above all from the Old Testament.

This Hebraistic tradition was characteristic of Protestant culture and has often been regarded, e.g. by Matthew Arnold, as responsible for the anti-humanist, Philistine character of middle-class culture in England and America. It was naturally strongest among the sects whose whole intellectual life was nourished on the Bible and the Bible only. But even in representatives of the highest Protestant culture, like Milton, there is a hard core of unassimilated Hebraism which is in conflict with their humanist education and which in lesser men produced a sharp dualism between religion and culture. It was this dualism which prevented the development of religious drama and religious art in the seventeenth century and caused that partial secularization of culture which destroyed the medieval unity of religious and social life.

In Catholic Europe, this was not so. As I have said, the Baroque culture was not confined to the scholars and the men of letters. It permeated the life of the people as a whole through the religious art and music and drama which continued to play the same part in the Baroque world as they had done in the Middle Ages.

Thus the drama instead of being banned by the Church was used deliberately as a means of religious instruction, so that in Spain, for example, religious and secular dramas were composed by the same authors, many of them priests, performed by the same actors and applauded by the same audiences. In the same way there was no sharp dualism in Catholic Europe between Christian and humanist ethics.

The synthesis of Catholic and Aristotelian ethics which was perhaps the most important of all the achievements of St. Thomas remained the basis of Catholic teaching and provided an ideal foundation for the creation of a Christian humanism which could integrate the moral values of the humanist tradition with the transcendent spiritual ends of Christian theology.

In Protestant Europe the influence of humanist ethics is considerable, as we can see in the Cambridge Platonists. Nevertheless the influence of the Old Testament was far stronger, especially in Calvinist countries, and it was this Hebraist ethos which explains both the strength and the weakness of Protestant culture. Alike in Calvin's Geneva and in Puritan New England, among Cromwell's Ironsides and among the Scottish Covenanters it produced a type of character and a way of life that were harsh and unattractive when judged by humanist standards but were as hard as iron and as irresistible as a steam hammer. This was the spiritual power behind the new economic order which was destined to transform Europe and the world. Against the rich communal life of Baroque Europe with its external magnificence and its internal poverty, its palaces and its monasteries, its saints and its beggars, there arose a society of godly merchants and shopkeepers and craftsmen who worked hard and spent little, who regarded themselves as God's elect, and who were ready to fight to the death against any attempt of king or bishop to interfere with their religion or their business.

No two forms of European culture could have been more different and more irreconcilable with one another. And yet both of them were intensely religious, and both alike were equally hostile, though in different ways, to the seculariza-tion of culture which was the dominant characteristic of the eighteenth century. In fact this process of secularization did not originate with either of them. It had its source in a third type of culture which was intermediate between the Baroque and the Calvinist worlds and which I shall discuss in the next chapter.

3

Rationalism and Revolution

WHEN one considers the progress of the Catholic revival in the sixteenth and seventeenth centuries and the apparent strength of religious faith and practice both in Catholic and Protestant Europe at that time, it is difficult to understand how European culture ever became secularized. In the middle of the seventeenth century Europe, and America also, were divided between opposing forms of religion and culture, but both of them—the Baroque culture of the South and the Protestant culture of the North—were intensely religious and sincerely Christian. Yet in a century or a century and a half all this was changed and Europe had become the Europe that we know. Religion had become a matter of private opinion and the public life of the state and the intellectual community of culture had become almost completely secularized.

This change was even more revolutionary than that of the sixteenth century, although it was less spectacular. For it was not the result of the French Revolution. The spiritual revolution had been already accomplished before there was any question of a political one.

How then are we to explain so vast a change? It was not, as is sometimes supposed, the direct consequence of the Reformation, nor was it due to the political or cultural victory of the Protestant North over the Catholic South. Yet on the other hand its had no roots within the Baroque culture itself, for the latter had attained a state of social and political equilibrium which might have endured for centuries, if it had not been disturbed from without. Spain and Italy were as impervious to Protestantism as Scotland and Scandinavia were impervious to Catholicism. And so too in America there was no possibility of mutual influence or understanding between the Protestants of New England and the Catholics of New France or New Spain.

But to this rule there was one great exception. Throughout the decisive period in which the new Catholic and Protestant cultures were becoming stabilized, the largest national state in Western Europe remained divided between the two religions. The French religious wars of the sixteenth century had ended in a kind of stalemate by which the leader of the Protestants became the representative of French national unity by himself becoming a Catholic, while at the same time guaranteeing the rights and privileges of the Protestant minority. The Edict of Nantes not only secured freedom of conscience for the Protestants; it recognized their corporate existence as an organized society—a state within a state—with their own religious and political assemblies, their own fortresses and practically their own army.

Nevertheless these very generous terms did not represent a Protestant triumph, but rather a victory for the party of conciliation, the so-called Politiques, who were prepared to sacrifice the principle of religious unity to the cause of national unity and who found their leader and representative in Henry IV himself, who repeatedly changed his religion according to political circumstances; once insincerely in order to save his life after the massacre of St. Bartholomew and once with apparent sincerity at the moment when his conversion gave him the crown and defeated the European hegemony of Spanish Catholicism.

For Henry IV the re-establishment of national unity after forty years of civil war was the first essential. If his subjects were good Frenchmen they could be Catholic or Protestant, but they must be Frenchmen first. And this point of view made a strong appeal to a generation which had been ruined by the miseries of civil war, deafened by religious controversy and touched in their national pride by foreign intervention. They welcomed the restoration of the royal power as an impartial arbiter which would be strong enough to impose peace on the rival Churches and parties which were tearing France in pieces. It is true that the age of Henry IV and Richelieu witnessed a great movement of Catholic revival which produced a galaxy of saints and mystics, like the Spanish revival in the previous century. But unlike the latter it was not a universal movement which embraced and inspired the whole culture, but a minority movement, which like the Puritan movement in England was a protest against the secularizing tendencies of the national culture. This analogy with Puritanism is especially visible on the left wing of the French Catholic revival which is represented by the Jansenist movement and which contributed no less than Protestantism itself to the loss of religious unity and to the growth of a sectarian spirit.

Meanwhile the work of Henry IV was being carried on

by Cardinal Richelieu, the classical representative of the *raison d'état,* who did more than Gustavus Adolphus or Cromwell to defeat the international policy of the Counter Reformation and to destroy the political unity of Catholic Europe. And this ruthless system of international power-politics which established the greatness of France on the ruin of Central Europe went hand in hand with an equally ruthless system of internal centralization which prepared the way for the absolute national monarchy of Louis XIV.

The effects of this revolution were not only political; they were also religious and cultural. The Gallican Church became more and more an autonomous ecclesiastical organism and French culture became progressively detached from the Baroque culture of Catholic Europe. This new national culture still shared the ideals of the humanist culture, but instead of applying them, as the Baroque society had done, to the service of an international religion, it used culture, in the Augustan manner, as an instrument of government and empire. This ideal found its most complete expression in the palace of Versailles and the elaborate ritual of the court of Louis XIV. All the resources of the nation were concentrated on the worship of the Roi Soleil whose splendour in turn was reflected by every facet of French culture. As Racine himself said in one of his discourses to the Academy, "All the words of the language, and even the syllables, seem precious to us because we regard them as so many instruments with which to serve the glory of our august protector."

Accordingly literature and art were subjected to a strict social regime, administered by the various royal academies: the Academie Française, the Academie des Sciences, the

Academie des Beaux Arts, and the rest. There was no longer any room for the unbridled fantasy and spiritual ecstasy of the Baroque genius. The watch-words of the new culture were order and regularity, good taste and good sense, reason and clear ideas. Its spirit was essentially classical but it was also rationalist, and this rationalist element gradually permeated the whole culture until it undermined and ultimately destroyed the authoritarian orthodoxy of the Gallican Church and the authoritarian absolutism of the French monarchy.

The source of this rationalist tradition was, however, quite distinct from that of the academic classical culture. For at the same time that Richelieu was reorganizing the political and social order according to the principle of the *raison d'état*, another great man, Descartes, was reorganizing the world of thought according to abstract mathematical principles. He was essentially a revolutionary genius who made a clean sweep of authority and tradition and created a new intellectual world by the unaided powers of individual reason. And yet there was a profound affinity—and even a spiritual identity—between the rationalism of this most independent of thinkers who lived in voluntary exile in Holland and the spirit of the new classical culture. So that in spite of the opposition of all the vested interests in the Church and the Universities, the Cartesian movement won the support not only of the scientific world but of all the leaders of French culture and French religion with the partial exception of Pascal—whether they were Gallicans like Bossuet, Jansenists like Arnauld and Nicole, or mystics like Malebranche.

Nevertheless the transcendental ontological aspect of Descartes' philosophy, which explains its religious appeal, was not the element that was the most influential or the most enduring. As Fontenelle wrote, it was not the metaphysics of Descartes but his new method of reasoning that was the important thing. The ordinary educated man for whom Fontenelle was the spokesman could make nothing of Malebranche's "vision of all things in God" or even of Descartes' proof of the necessity for the Divine existence, but he was very sensible of the value of clear ideas and of the importance of submitting received opinions and beliefs to strict rational criticism. There is, after all, a democratic and anti-authoritarian principle explicit in the new Cartesian method. Does he not begin his discourse by asserting that "Good sense is of all things in the world the most widely distributed" and that "good sense is by nature equal in all men"? And it was this universal appeal not to the trained intelligence of the philosopher but to the good sense of the ordinary man that was the great characteristic of the eighteenth century when the French classical culture and the new "philosophic" ideas were alike diffused from one end of Europe to the other through the cosmopolitan society of the courts and the salons.

Nor was this development confined to Catholic Europe, for a parallel movement was taking place in England, which destroyed the religious unity of Protestant culture and prepared the way for its secularization. In England as in France the nation had gone through a period of civil and religious strife which had made men look for some principle of unity that stood outside the field of theological controversy. As

the religious wars in France had discredited both the Hugue-
nots and the Catholic League, so the English Civil Wars
had discredited the intransigence both of the Puritans and
of their Episcopalian opponents. But in England, unlike
France, the monarchy itself had been defeated. Strafford,
who might have been the English Richelieu, had lost his
head. So too had Charles I, and though the act of regicide
had shocked the popular conscience, it dealt a blow to the
doctrine of Divine Right from which the English monarchy
never entirely recovered. Henceforth the English people
sought a middle way which it found, after a very unrevolu-
tionary Revolution, in a regime of limited monarchy and
limited religious toleration combined with unlimited individualism and freedom of thought.

This English solution was exactly the opposite to that of
France, and the two nations were involved for twenty-seven
years in almost continuous war. Yet in spite of their national
and political differences both English and French culture
show a similar reaction against mysticism and religious "enthusiasm" and a similar trend towards science and rationalism.

It is true that there is a sharp contrast between the geo-
metrical reason of Descartes and the empirical common
sense of Locke, which reflects the difference in spirit of the
two cultures. Nevertheless these two schools of thought met
and mingled with one another in the culture of the Enlightenment. The philosophy of Voltaire and the Encyclopaedists
was that of Locke rather than of Descartes. Yet the driving
force behind it is still the Cartesian rationalism with its sublime confidence in the infallibility of reason, its dissolvent

criticism of received beliefs and traditions, and its determination "never to accept anything for true which I did not clearly know to be such."

Thus the spiritual barrier which divided the two post-Reformation cultures of Catholic and Protestant Europe was broken down, not by the victory of one over the other but by the weakening of religious convictions before the self-confident, superficial rationalism of the new lay intelligentsia.

Other factors besides philosophical ones contributed to the breaking down of the cultural frontier between the Catholic and Protestant worlds at the close of the seventeenth century. Above all the Revocation of the Edict of Nantes and the expulsion or forcible conversion of the French Protestants had the opposite effect to that which Louis XIV intended. For the Protestant exiles who swarmed into Holland and England in their thousands acted at once as the disseminators of French culture and as propagandists for the cause of religious toleration and political liberty. There has never been a body of *emigrés* so intellectually active and so socially influential as the Huguenot exiles. In England they provided the translators, like Abel Boyer, Des Maiseaux, Pierre Coste, Peter Motteux, and the rest, who acted as intermediaries between English and Continental culture. In Holland, which was the chief centre of the emigration, they became the founders of international journalism, and the French reviews and encyclopaedias which poured from the Dutch printing presses had an enormous influence on European opinion. The famous Dictionary which was published by the greatest of these Huguenot publicists, Pierre Bayle, in

1695–7 was more widely read than any work of the kind. It became the freethinker's vade mecum and prepared the way for the work of Voltaire and the Encyclopaedists.

Moreover, it must not be forgotten that the Huguenot exiles still possessed a large body of secret sympathizers inside France among the ex-Protestants and crypto-Protestants who had become nominally Catholic under the stress of persecution. It is, of course, difficult to determine the exact influence of this factor in the secularization of French culture, since in the nature of the case it was a subterranean and to some extent an unconscious influence, but it was certainly of considerable importance owing to the position that the Protestant middle classes had held in economics and professional life. In any case, it was largely owing to the work of the French Protestant exiles that the new secular culture acquired a cosmopolitan character. This culture was still French in spirit and ideals, but it was no longer identified, as in the seventeenth century, with the power of the French monarchy and the political expansion of French power.

Nevertheless it was still limited to the three northwestern countries—France, Holland and England—with a somewhat uneven extension into north and west Germany. The Baroque culture of southern and central Europe still remained a closed world, and owing to the authoritarian character of the governments and the control of the Church over education and literature, the new culture and the new ideas had little opportunity of infiltration.

But it so happened that at this moment at the turn of the century a great change took place on the political level which entirely altered the balance of European culture. The extinction of the Hapsburg dynasty in Spain and the War of the Spanish Succession suddenly brought Spain and Spanish America under the rule of the Bourbons and broke the connection between Spain and Austria which had played an important part in the history of the Counter Reformation and the rise of the Baroque culture.

At first sight it may seem surprising that a mere change of dynasty should have any deep effect on a nation that was so jealous of its independence and so fiercely attached to its national and religious traditions as Spain. But though the spirit of the people was unchanged, the Spanish government in the later seventeenth century was in a state of such extreme disorder and impotence as to create a vacuum in the centre of the political organism. Into this vacuum there came a foreign dynasty and a new government which were naturally French in sympathy and were forced to rely on the power and prestige of Louis XIV in order to establish themselves.

Thus the eighteenth century in Spain was characterized by the predominance of foreign influences. The Spanish court became a satellite of Versailles, like so many European courts of the period, and the way was open for the penetration of new men, new manners and new ideas into the very centre of national life. The result was a breach in the continuity of Spanish culture which led to the divorce of Spain from her old connections with Austria and Baroque Europe and which incorporated her artificially and externally in the new international society of French culture with which she had no organic historical relation. The Spanish people remained faithful to their old spiritual ideals and cultural traditions, but these could no longer influence the course of history as they lacked intellectual and political leadership. Thus there arose that dualism between the Gallicized culture of the ruling classes and the traditional culture of the common people which was to endure for two centuries and which produced such catastrophic results in later history. The classical French culture of the *Grand Siècle* and still more that of the eighteenth-century Enlightenment had neither sympathy nor understanding for the ideals of the Baroque culture, and this antipathy led to a general depreciation of Spanish achievements and traditions which gradually infected the mind of the educated classes in Spain itself and produced that sense of inferiority which became characteristic of the *afrancesados* and liberals of the later eighteenth and early nineteenth centuries.

Nor is this surprising when we consider the changes that had taken place in Spain's international position. In the world of the Baroque culture Spain had always possessed a pre-eminent position, not merely on account of her political power but owing to the spiritual prestige of her saints and mystics and theologians. But in the new culture of the Enlightenment these spiritual achievements counted for nothing and less than nothing. Spanish culture had to start afresh as a backward pupil of the philosophers and economists whose whole scale of values contradicted that on which Spain's former greatness had been founded.

The extent to which this disavowal of the past went is to be seen in the part which Spain took in the destruction of the Society of Jesus (1767)—the event which marks the end of the great period of modern Catholic culture which had begun at the Council of Trent. Even in France the destruction of the Society (1764) was an act of political irresponsibility which was contrary to the true interests of the French monarchy. But in Spain it was much more than this: it was a suicidal act which ran counter to the whole national tradition and destroyed the keystone of the common spiritual culture which had formerly united Spain with Baroque Europe and which still united Spain with her colonial Empire.

Meanwhile in central Europe the Baroque culture still remained alive and active. Indeed the last decades of the seventeenth century and the first half of the eighteenth century were the great age of the Austrian Baroque. This was the age that saw the reconquest of Hungary and Croatia from the Turks, the final defeat of the advance of Islam into eastern Europe and the re-Catholicizing of the Danubian lands under Leopold II and Charles VI. It was also the golden age of German Baroque art, when the great monasteries and pilgrimage churches of architects like the Dietzenhofers, Prandauer, Fischer von Erlach, Baltasar Neumann and Dominikus Zimmerman were arising all over central Europe. If religious art and architecture and music are any indication, there can be no question of the vitality of Austro-German Catholic culture in the eighteenth century. Nevertheless this culture was the final product of a European movement which was already a thing of the past, and it could not survive the loss of its international background.

Consequently in the second half of the eighteenth century it came to an abrupt end, and Germany accepted the Enlightenment as suddenly and completely as she had accepted the Reformation two centuries earlier.

The transformation of German culture was due to a double movement which operated simultaneously from without and from within, from above and from below. (1) On the one hand, there was the direct influence of the French Enlightenment which acted through the courts and the rulers, like Frederick II of Prussia and Joseph II of Austria; (2) on the other, there was the awakening of German Protestant culture which created a new literature and a new philosophy. It was this, far more than any political change, which made the German middle classes conscious of their national unity and of their social importance, and this new spirit of cultural nationalism was transmitted not only to Catholic South Germany, but also to the non-German peoples of the East, like the Czechs and the Magyars, who had hitherto shared in the international unity of Baroque culture which was Latin rather than German in origin.

It was this combination of rational enlightenment and romantic nationalism which broke down the traditional order of Church and State in both Catholic and Protestant Europe and caused the complete secularization of Western culture.

The leaders of the Enlightenment were fully conscious of the revolutionary character of their work, and all through the middle decades of the eighteenth century they were carrying on a regular campaign of propaganda which was primarily directed against the Catholic Church as the arch-enemy of the Enlightenment.

In 1765 Voltaire wrote to Helvetius: "Do you not see that

the whole of Northern Europe is on our side and that sooner or later the base fanatics of the South must be confounded? The Empress of Russia, the King of Poland, the King of Prussia, conqueror of superstitious Austria, and many other princes have raised the banner of philosophy. During the last twelve years there has been a perceptible revolution in men's minds. . . . The light is certainly spreading in all directions." (Voltaire, *Lettres* VI:X)

No doubt Voltaire neither foresaw nor desired the revolution that was actually to come. He even says in the letter I have just quoted: "I well know that the established hierarchy will not be destroyed, for the people needs one." Nevertheless the destructive criticisms of the philosophers had undermined the order of Christian culture more completely than they realized, and it only needed the coming of a dynamic emotional impulse which appealed to the masses for the revolution to become a social and political reality. This element was supplied by Rousseau and his disciples, who found in the democratic ideology of *the rights of man* and the *national will* a new faith strong enough to inspire a new social and political order.

The theories of Rousseau had the same relation to the ideology of the Jacobin party as the theories of Karl Marx to the ideology of communism. Indeed there is a genetic relation between them, since the history of the modern revolutionary movement has been a continuous one, so that democracy, nationalism, socialism and communism are all of them successive or simultaneous aspects of the same process. Thus there is a socialist element in the thought of a typical nationalist like Fichte, a democratic element in Marx and a nationalist element in Stalin.

In the same way we can see in all these movements, with the partial exception of nationalism, the influence of the eighteenth-century Enlightenment. This continuity with eighteenth-century ideas is to be seen most clearly in the case of European Liberalism, which is simply the continuation of the Enlightenment in the nineteenth century and its adaptation to the conditions of capitalist society. But socialism and communism have also remained faithful in their fashion to the belief in human progress and perfectibility and in the boundless powers of human reason and science which characterized the eighteenth century. Marx himself regarded the philosophical achievement of the Enlightenment as no less important than the political achievement of the Revolution and goes so far as to say that even developed communism derives directly from French eighteenth-century materialism.

How is this ideological view of the European revolution to be reconciled with the economic interpretation of history? In Marx's view the intellectual and the political revolution were essentially one and both were based on the economic revolution and the rise of bourgeois capitalism. And the attention of Marx was so concentrated on this last factor, especially in its industrial phase, that he tended to ignore or underestimate all the factors which did not square with his theory. Nevertheless, to anyone who studies the history of the process as a whole, it is obvious that throughout the greater part of Europe the intellectual and religious changes which produced the secularization of Western culture preceded the economic revolution and were not produced by it.

In Germany and throughout Eastern Europe, as well as in Italy and Spain, the agents of change were not the new capitalist *bourgeoisie* but the old professional middle class, the men of letters and the professors, the lawyers and the government officials. Even in France, where economic conditions were more advanced, the capitalists who played a part in the Enlightenment were not the industrial capitalists but chiefly the "Farmers General" and the government contractors who represented a tradition as ancient as the *publicani* of the Roman Republic.

As in Russia so in Europe generally it was the intelligentsia, the class to which Marx himself belonged, and not the capitalists or the proletariat who were the real agents of change and the source of the revolutionary tradition.

The other essential factor was the political organization which these classes served—*the State:* not the popular state of the democratic ideology, but the new model of centralized absolutism which had been created by Richelieu and Louis XIV (or rather his ministers) and which had been imitated and developed by the "enlightened despots" of the following century—Peter the Great and Frederick the Great and Catherine the Great and their followers.

This affinity and collaboration between an "enlightened" intelligentsia and an enlightened despotism still persists in the Marxian tradition of the revolutionary intelligentsia and the revolutionary dictatorship, and today it has reached its ultimate conclusion in the totalitarian absolutism of Soviet Communism in which the police state and the ideological party have become fused with one another and where every aspect of culture is submitted to a process of strict psychological conditioning and control in the interest of a dogmatic secularist ideology. But today this movement is no longer a characteristically Western and European one. More and more it is passing over to Asia and becoming identified with the reaction of oriental nationalism against Western predominance and European culture.

Under these conditions what are the prospects of Western culture? It is impossible to go any further on the road of revolution and secularism which has been followed for so long, for this road has reached its ultimate conclusion. Only two alternatives remain. We can either remain in the halfway house of liberal democracy, striving desperately to maintain the higher standards of economic life which are the main justification of our secularized culture; or we can return to the tradition on which Europe was founded and set about the immense task of the restoration of Christian culture.

However difficult this task may seem to be, it is not an impossible one, for the most difficult part of it has already been accomplished: the almost miraculous survival of Christianity in a secularized culture. Two hundred years ago Christian culture was in a state of extreme decadence which affected the life of the Church itself and for which there seemed to be no human remedy. The destruction of the Society of Jesus by the action of the Catholic monarchies and the confirmation of their work by the Papacy itself marked not only the defeat of Catholicism as an international force but the self-acceptance of that defeat; and the subsequent action of the Revolution in the dechristianization of France and the secularization of the European order was only the logical completion of this process. But from that moment the tide began to turn. In comparison with the eighteenth

century, the nineteenth century was an age of Catholic revival, which witnessed the restoration of the religious orders,
the revival of Christian education and Christian philosophy
and a new expansion of missionary activity. Above all the
Church reasserted its independence of the State and became
more than ever before a completely autonomous and unified
international society.

Now if all this was achieved against the spirit of the age,
in face of the triumphant progress of secular civilization, it
should surely be far easier to carry the process of restoration
a stage further into the sphere of culture and social life, at a
time when the hopes of secular progress have been so bitterly
disappointed.

At the same time we must not forget that the Catholic
revival of the nineteenth century was rendered possible by
the survival of a living Christian tradition among the masses,
whereas today secularism has penetrated deeply into the
popular consciousness. The problem that we are facing
today is therefore quite unlike that which confronted the
Church in the post-Reformation period. Our position is
more like that of the Christians under the Roman Empire,
when the Church had on the one hand to convert the pagan
masses in the great Mediterranean cities, Antioch and Ephe-
sus and Rome, and at the same time to defend its bare right
to exist against the crushing weight of an all-powerful world
state which recognized no limits to its authority.

THE WORLD EXPANSION
OF WESTERN CULTURE

4

The Missionary Expansion of Western Christendom

THE position of Christianity in the world today has been rarely considered by modern historians. It is none the less a question of central importance for the understanding of modern civilization. For twelve centuries Christianity has been the religion of a culture—that is to say, it has had an organic relation with the social and moral structure of one particular society of peoples. It has held somewhat the same place in Europe that Islam has held in Western Asia, Hinduism in India, or Confucianism in China. It has been the official creed of Western man; it has moulded his institutions, ruled his education and either created or influenced his moral values and his spiritual ideals. During the last two centuries the bonds of this organic union have been loosened and modern civilization has been progressively detached from its religious roots. Yet at the same time this has not involved the disappearance of Christianity as a living religion—on the contrary, these centuries have witnessed a remarkable expansion of Christianity throughout the world, an expansion which is partly due to direct missionary activity and partly to the extension of Western civilization across the Atlantic and the colonization of the empty spaces of the world by peoples of European stock and Christian tradition.

What is the significance of this twofold and apparently contradictory process? Is this modern expansion of Christianity merely the religious aspect of the world hegemony achieved by Western civilization in the eighteenth and nineteenth centuries? Or does it portend the advent of a new and truly world-wide Christendom in which Christianity will achieve a new organic relation with the world civilization of the future?

There is much to be said for each of these alternatives, but hitherto the question has never been adequately discussed. In particular, there have been few attempts to study the expansion of Christianity in the last one hundred and fifty years, apart from Professor Latourette's massive seven-volume *History of the Expansion of Christianity*.

First of all we must recognize the ambivalent character of the nineteenth century. This period has seldom been regarded as a great religious age, and has more often been viewed as an irreligious century, the age which saw the passing of the old order in Church and State and the birth of the new scientific and industrial civilization. Yet there are some, like Professor Latourette, who take a very different point of view. For them the nineteenth century was pre-eminently an age of hope and unlimited opportunity for spiritual as well as material achievement. And it is certainly true that it has only been in the last century and a half that Christianity, for the first time in its history, transcended the limits of a particular culture and became a world-wide movement which reached every continent, and almost every people and language.

In the nineteenth century this expansion was very closely linked with the colonial and economic expansion of the Western peoples—so closely that it has often been regarded as the same process in a religious form. In the present century, however, under the impact of the new non-occidental nationalist movements, the connection between Christianity and the expansion of the West has been weakened. The leadership in the missionary Churches is passing from the foreigner to the native element. But at the same time the advance of Christianity has continued with increasing intensity. In the last thirty years the percentage of Christians among non-occidental peoples has been doubled or more than doubled in spite of the fact that the new political and social movements which have been characteristic of the age have been unfriendly or openly hostile to the Christian faith.

This in itself is a remarkable achievement, and at first sight it seems to justify the optimism with which some Christians face the prospect of the decline of the West. But it is as yet too soon to say whether the Christian penetration of the non-European world is profound or superficial. Our views on this question will depend on our view of the nineteenth-century development from which it sprang. And the degree of one's optimism will be especially determined by the judgment one passes on the specifically "Anglo-Saxon" type of Christianity which contributed so much materially, morally and culturally, to the great movement of expansion of missionary activity in the last one hundred and fifty years.

It is truly an astonishing record. The religion of the old

world, and especially the sectarian Christianity of the British Isles, was sown broadcast in the virgin soil of America, and produced new varieties which in turn were propagated round the world till they came back to Europe once more. The Schwenkfeldians, "the Confessors of the Glory of Christ," have vanished from their native Silesia and survive in Pennsylvania, while there are still disciples of the English prophetess Mother Anne Lee who maintain their strict community life in the State of Maine. On the other hand, the Seventh Day Adventists, who appeared as a tiny sect in New England in the middle of the nineteenth century, have expanded steadily in all directions, from China to Peru, until by the middle of this century they had reached two hundred and ninety-five lands and five hundred and four languages. And the same intense missionary activity is shown by the other sects of American origin, such as the Mormons, the Christian Scientists and the body that is known as "Jehovah's Witnesses."

No doubt none of these bodies is representative of the main tradition of American Christianity. All, however, possess the missionary impulse and the power of expansion which is lacking in some of the more classical types of American Protestantism, notably in the case of the Unitarians, the Church of William Ellery Channing and Emerson, which has made such a considerable contribution to American religion and life.

In reading the history of the geographical expansion of Christianity, we cannot be satisfied with quantitative standards. At every stage we are faced with the problem of quality, with the nature of the religion which is diffused and the character of the men who are diffusing it. At every stage we must ask, what was it that spread? By what processes did it spread? What effect did it have on its new environment and vice versa? And why has the process of expansion some-times been arrested or reversed? But it is not easy to answer these questions. Indeed nowhere is the apparent irrationality of history more apparent than in this field. Why was the Church of Cyprian and Augustine extinguished in North Africa, while the Church of Abyssinia survives to this day? Why did the Pitcairn Islanders become Seventh Day Ad-ventists, and the Tonga Islanders Wesleyans? Why have the flourishing Nestorian Churches of Eastern Asia disappeared except in Malabar, where it is no longer Nestorian but Monophysite? These are historical accidents, like the sur-vival of Buddhism in the Nogai Steppes in Russia or the Albanian Uniats of Southern Italy.

But we need some deeper and more universal cause to explain the steady westward trend of Christianity and the fact that the great modern expansion has been almost solely by its two Western forms, Roman Catholic and Protestant. For it is at first sight most surprising that the reaction of oriental nationalism against the West has brought no expan-sion to the Eastern forms of Christianity; it is from the Western Missions, and especially those of America, that the new Christendom of the Far East and of Africa is derived. Sun Yat-sen was the pupil of the Anglicans. The Soong fam-ily and Chiang Kai-shek were Methodists of the American denomination. Even in Japan, where the conflict with the West has been sharpest in the past; where the government had done all in its power to incorporate the Christians into the totalitarian national community before the collapse of the Japanese Empire in 1945; the influence of Western Christianity remained strong, and Toyohiko Kagawa, who was an outstanding figure in the Christian national movement, was characteristically Western in his religious approach to the social problem.

No doubt this expansion of Western Christianity owed much to the political and economic expansion of Western civilization. But this is not the whole explanation. It was due even more to the inner vitality of the forces of Christianity which had found a new social expression in the changed environment of the new world. In the English-speaking world during the last two centuries Christianity has been free to develop in its own way by its own resources without state control or political interference. In other words, the pattern of Church and State as fixed by the legislators of the later Roman Empire and the Carolingians was replaced by a new type of voluntary organization which has provided the pattern for the new Churches of the new non-European world. Yet at the same time there was no complete break with the past, and the Churches of America remained in full communion with their parent Churches of the old world.

At first sight this development seemed to mark the victory of the Protestant over the Catholic type of Christianity. But, as the nineteenth century proceeded, it was seen that this was not the case, and in the twentieth century it became clear that the Catholic Church was not only able to adapt itself to the new pattern, but actually derived fresh strength and energy from the changed conditions. This is shown most strikingly in the United States themselves, where Catholicism began as the unpopular religion of a minute and unprivileged alien minority and where it has grown until it is by far the largest and most powerful of the American denominations, numbering far more than the combined total of the Congregationalists, the Episcopalians and the Presbyterians, who between them represent the older traditions of American religion.

A similar situation is to be found in the Far East, Australia and Africa, where the absence of state support seems to stimulate rather than check the advance of Christianity. Here also the nineteenth century was the great age of Protestant expansion, while in the twentieth century the advance of Catholicism has been even more rapid. And the result has been that, as Professor Latourette remarks, "For the first time in its history Christianity was becoming really worldwide and not a colonial or imperial extension, ecclesiastically speaking, of an Occidental faith. Indeed in this it was unique. No other religion has ever achieved such world-embracing dimensions. We may go farther and say that no set of ideas, not even the widely propagated Communism of the period, had ever been so extensively represented by organized groups or so rooted among so many different peoples."[1]

This advance of Christianity into new fields has, however, been accompanied by a recession in Christendom itself, where the old type of a society that was traditionally and culturally Christian has been destroyed or threatened by the

---

[1] *History of the Expansion of Christianity* (New York, Harper and Brothers), vol. vii, p. 411.

rise of the totalitarian state and the drastic secularization of society and culture. The overt persecution of religion in Communist Russia and, in the past, in Nazi Germany, may be a transitory phenomenon, but the tendency to the secularization of culture is continuous and universal and there is no sign of any return to the ideal of a positive Christian culture, such as Mr. T. S. Eliot has described in his *Idea of a Christian Society*. Everywhere Christians, whether Orthodox, Roman Catholic or Protestant, are tending to be self-conscious minorities set in an alien or hostile world.

This trend has been undoubtedly strengthened by the catastrophic events of the last few decades which have shown how fragile is the barrier which separates the highest material civilization from the lowest depths of destructiveness and inhumanity. Already in the years between the two world wars there was a strong tendency to reject the liberal optimism of nineteenth-century Protestantism in favor of the uncompromising Barthian theology of crisis which has had such a wide influence on religious thought both in Europe and America. This tendency has been even more accentuated by the destructive effects of World War II and the threat of atomic warfare which now hangs over the world. The result has been to discredit, in some degree at least, that alliance of the forces of religious idealism and humanitarian reform which contributed so much to Protestant missionary activity from the time of Wilberforce and Buxton to that of the Christian Student Movement and the Universal Christian Council for Life and Work. At the same time the field of voluntary social activity has been restricted, and in some cases completely closed, by the extension of state action and the determination of the totalitarian socialist and nationalist parties to control every possible channel of social influence. This determination of the modern secularist, either to confine the Church to the sacristy or to use it as the obedient servant of the totalitarian state, threatens the freedom of Christian life to a degree in which it has never been threatened before.

The problems involved by this new situation have as yet not been fully realized by public opinion, except in reference to some particular conflict. Yet it is clear that even though National Socialism has been destroyed and Communism seems to have adopted a new policy towards religion, these problems will remain, and must have a profound effect on the expansion of Christianity. It is too soon to say whether they will produce a major recession of Christianity which will counterbalance the gains of the last century and a half, or whether they point towards a situation like that of the early centuries of our era, when Christianity first developed its world mission as a vigorous and persecuted underground movement.

It is impossible to give a confident answer to these questions, for the forces that are involved are too unpredictable and mysterious. Nevertheless, if one's personal sympathies are with the new voluntary type of missionary Christianity, rather than with the traditional European pattern of hereditary Christian culture, the prospect of a shifting of the centre of gravity from Europe to the non-European world will not seem an alternative greatly to be feared. And there are, moreover, new grounds of hope for the Protestant in the trend towards unity which during the last fifty years has increasingly taken the place of the fissiparous tendency which for centuries seemed inseparable from Protestantism, most of all perhaps in the United States. It seems, in fact, as though the sectarian principle had worked itself out, and that a new form of ecclesiastical unity is being gradually built up in the Protestant world. This movement has taken two forms. In the first place there has been the creation of United Protestant Churches, such as the United Church of Canada formed in 1925 by the coming together of the Methodists, the Congregationalists and the Presbyterians, the Church of Christ in China, constituted in 1927, and the Church of Christ in Japan, in 1941. In the second place there is the Ecumenical Movement, which is federal and co-operative in spirit and world-wide in scope and which has found its organ in the World Council of the Churches.

No doubt there is a wide difference of opinion with regard to the importance of this movement. There are some who see in it a sign of flagging energies and a decline of the religious individualism which sprouted so vigorously in a hundred sects. Nor is there any sign that it is likely to bridge the gap between Protestant and Catholic Christianity, and to bring the whole Christian world into a single religious community. Some leaders of the World Council look forward rather to the development of two world-wide Christian societies, organized not against one another, but against a godless and secularist world. Certainly the rise of the Ecumenical Movement has not increased the antagonism between Catholicism and Protestantism, which is actually strongest in those sects which have held most aloof from it. Nevertheless the conception of a world Christianity permanently and consciously organized on a dualistic basis is one which is obviously unsatisfactory from many points of view—most of all from its incompatibility with the fundamental Christian concept of the one Body, the importance of which is realized today by every school of theological thought more clearly than at any time in the past.

Everywhere we are witnessing a return to corporate ways of thought and action, a new realization of the religious significance of the community and an increasing interest in the expression of collective consciousnness in myth and ritual and art. This marks a great change from the individualism of nineteenth-century civilization, which characterized Westtern religion as well as secular culture, above all in Britain and America.

The great missionary expansion of the nineteenth century was everywhere based on the principle of individual conversion, and this is equally true of the internal development of Western religion which, as we see in all the most characteristic religious documents of the period, was marked by an introspective psychological approach and an intensely personal view of conversion and salvation. There is a fundamental contrast between this approach and the collective or communal form of expression which had dominated the Christian world for upwards of a thousand years. Western Christendom was not built up by the method of individual conversions. It was a way of life which the people accepted as a whole, often by the decision of their rulers, and which when accepted affected the whole life of society by the change of their institutions and laws. It is easy to condemn this type of corporate Christianity as superficial, external or subchristian, but at least it means that Christianity is accepted as a social fact which affects every side of life and not merely as an opinion or a specialized group activity or even as a hobby. Nor can we assume that the kings and bishops who laid the foundations of Western Christendom were less in earnest or less genuinely Christian than the leaders of modern sectarian Christianity. If the former shared the weakness of the barbarian culture from which they sprang, the latter have often been no less affected by the influence of the commercial and competitive civilization in which they lived. Moreover it may well be claimed that the missionary Churches of the Dark Ages produced a richer harvest even in the sphere of culture than anything that the modern missionary movement can show. There is little in the new non-occidental Christianity that can be compared with Bede and Boniface, with the religious art of Northumbria or with the new vernacular Christian literature. For in the case of Anglo-Saxon England, the mass conversion of the people meant the rebirth of culture, whereas too often the modern system of individual and competitive conversion has involved the piecemeal disintegration of native culture. There is surely something to be said for the view of the anthropologists who believe that every culture, even the most primitive, has a right to exist, and that a way of life which has been slowly and painfully evolved by a particular people to meet the needs of its particular environment has a value and significance for that people which nothing else can supply. If such a people is suddenly and completely transformed by their translation into an entirely different cultural world, they stand to lose more than they gain.

On the other hand, the alternative of protecting the culture of the simpler peoples from violent disruption while introducing them gradually into a wider moral and spiritual community has much to commend it. For it preserves the true essence of cultural nationalism, which is the instinctive loyalty that every people feels for its traditional cultural values, while subordinating it to the universal moral values which are the essence of a higher civilization.

The instantaneous switch-over from the total isolation of primitive barbarism to total integration in the modern world-society imposes an unbearable strain alike on human nature and on the way of life of a simple society. There must be an intermediate stage of education and acclimatization, and this stage is provided by the Christian missions better than by the nationalistic movements which promise too much and give too little.

It is true that modern missionaries are becoming increasingly conscious of their responsibilities in this respect, and are making a positive effort to avoid the disruption of native culture and to adapt their teaching to the indigenous forms of thought and social structure. But this is a very recent movement which is part of that return to corporate ways of thought to which we have just referred. In some cases, as in Polynesia and many parts of Africa, it has come too late to prevent the disintegration of culture, while elsewhere it is in danger of being overwhelmed by the rising tide of oriental nationalism which is apt to regard Christian missions as a form of Western imperialism. It is obvious that the new nationalism, with its superpolitical implications, must tend to strengthen the resistance of the oriental religions to Christianity regarded as a Western religion, and to missionaries as disseminators of Western culture. This tendency is strongest in India and in the Moslem world, where religion and culture are so closely linked that they seem to form an inseparable whole. It is less pronounced in China and Japan, where the relation of religion and culture are not so close, and where the situation is complicated by the competing claims of Communism, which is also a missionary movement. Everywhere, however, conditions are becoming adverse to the spirit of free religious enterprise which founded missions and schools and hospitals, supported by foreign contributions and staffed by foreign workers. The days of free trade in ideas are over.

The ideological character of oriental nationalism, like that of the totalitarian parties, makes it impossible to treat education or religion as neutral territory which can be left open to the free activity of independent religious organizations. Hence we are returning to a situation similar to that which existed in the Middle Ages, where men's beliefs are no longer a question of individual choice but of mass decisions.

The totalitarian ideologies advance today, as Islam did in the early Middle Ages, by a combination of military conquest and ideological propaganda. And Christianity is forced to face this challenge, not because it has a political character or seeks political power, but because the new ideologies seek to conquer and occupy the whole ground of community life, psychological as well as sociological. One should not identify Christianity simply with the traditional culture of Western Christendom, for it is the nature of

Christianity to transcend culture as it transcends nationality. But the sectarian Christianity of the nineteenth century avoided the difficulty because it was subcultural and unaware of the spiritual implications of culture, rather than because it was supercultural and able to embrace all peoples in the catholicity of a supranational bond of Faith.

5

The Spread of Western Ideologies

THE four great civilizations which constituted the world that we know were all spiritual communities that owed their unity to a common religion. In China, India, Islam and Christendom alike, political citizenship and racial origins were secondary to religious belief and practice. The Indian who ceased to observe the laws of caste and the worship of the gods and accepted the teaching of Mohammed ceased to be a Hindu and became a Moslem. And, in the same way, the western Moslem who became a Christian did not merely change his religion; he passed over from one civilization to another and acquired rights of citizenship in a new society.

During the last two centuries this situation has gradually changed. Nationality has taken the place of religion as the ultimate principle of social organization, and ideology has taken the place of theology as the creator of social ideals and the guide of public opinion. All over the world, beginning in Western Europe and extending gradually to the most remote regions of Asia and Africa, a change has taken place in the conditions of human existence and in the ways of social thought. The world has been made one, first by European trade, conquest and colonization, and later by Western science and technology. And behind the railway, the motor lorry and the airplane, there has spread a wave of secular ideas which had their origins in Europe in the age of the Enlightenment of the French Revolution, and which have communicated the ideas of political liberty and social equality, of nationality and self-determination from one people to another until they have become literally world-wide.

Although these ideas all had a common origin, during the nineteenth century they became differentiated into a number of distinct ideologies which were regarded as mutually exclusive and tended to become embodied in political parties and regimes. Thus Liberalism and Nationalism, Democracy and Socialism, Communism and Fascism all acquired this ideological form, although they were rarely found in a pure state. For example, we find National Liberalism and National Socialism in Germany, Liberal Democracy and Social Democracy in France and other similar compounds in other countries. At the present time there is a tendency for Liberal Democracy of the American type and Communist Socialism of the Russian type to become the opposite poles round which all the other ideologies and political regimes range themselves.

Thus we have two distinct ideological complexes, Western Democracy and Eastern Soviet Communism, which threaten to divide the world between them. Both of them are European, and even Western European in origin, but neither of them has its centre in Europe; one is Eurasian and the other is Euramerican. Both of them are secular ideologies as contrasted with the religious ideologies on which the four ancient world civilizations were based. Yet neither of them is entirely secular; Western Democracy is tending more and more to regard itself as the ally and protector of religion, while Soviet Communism, in spite of its avowedly anti-religious character, has always owed much of its success to its quasi-religious appeal. This is especially true in Asia, where Communism appears in the guise of a new religious or social way of salvation which promises to liberate men from oppression and suffering, on condition that they accept its authority and discipline by an act of unconditional surrender and obedience.

How does Europe stand in the face of this situation? Its position differs from both that of America and that of Asia. America has grown up with the new ideology. It can hardly conceive of a society which is not secular and democratic, since this is the only society it has known. In Asia, on the other hand, the movement of secularization is very recent and very alien to the traditions of Asiatic culture; indeed, it was only with the coming of Communism that the secular ideologies reached the masses and imparted a revolutionary momentum to the movement of social change. Even today in India, and even more in the Islamic world, the life of the people is still governed by religious beliefs and practices rather than by the secular ideologies.

In Europe, the ideologies are a native growth and have exercised a profound influence on European culture for at least two centuries. Nevertheless they have never completely destroyed the older tradition of Western Christendom, to which Europe owed its existence and its original sense of spiritual and cultural unity, and these two elements still exist today in a state of unstable equilibrium and tension. On the

Continent, Christian opinion has become organized through political parties and social programmes in the ideological pattern, so that it is sometimes regarded as one of the rival ideologies. In England, however, where this development has not occurred and where the political parties are strictly non-confessional, as in America, the pre-revolutionary tradition of the Christian state has never been officially disavowed, so that we still preserve the forms of a Christian monarchy and the legal establishment of the Christian Church.

What is the reason for this anomalous state of things which differentiates Europe from both America and Asia? There is no doubt that it is very deeply rooted in the history of the past and it seems to correspond to certain fundamental features of Western cultures. In the first place, I believe that the ideological diversity and tension of modern Europe is comparable to, and to some extent caused by, the religious diversity and tension of post-Reformation Europe. The theological disputes of the Reformation familiarized the masses with ideological issues, and the religious wars of the sixteenth and seventeenth centuries involved the same confusion of convictions, propaganda and power politics with which we are so familiar today. Moreover, the eighteenth century Enlightenment, the source of the modern ideological development, may be regarded historically as a kind of Second Reformation which in certain respects, as, for instance, in the destruction of the temporal power of the Church and the secularization of church property, carried out the work of the earlier Reformation in those parts of Europe which had previously been immune.

Owing to this long familiarity with internal conflict and

controversy, the impact of the new ideologies and the cold war of propaganda between opposing factions has been less devastating in Europe than elsewhere, since European culture can tolerate a much greater degree of internal tension than can other civilizations without losing its sense of continuity and community. This was largely due to the fact that in the past the opposing religions and ideologies of the West possessed a common origin and shared certain common principles and beliefs. Thus, in spite of their intense hostility to one another, Catholics and Protestants all regarded themselves as Christians, and the vast majority on both sides accepted the Bible and the Creeds, and appealed to the teachings of the Fathers in support of their respective principles. Even the theological controversies, which were the source of division, also led to the recognition of common positions and to alliances between different schools of thought, so that Lutherans could support Catholics in their controversy with the Socinians, and Jansenists could support Calvinists in their attack on the Arminians. While religious toleration was practically non-existent and freedom of thought was rare in either camp, a practical modus vivendi was worked out which made it possible for a Catholic like Descartes to live in Holland and Sweden and a Protestant like Leibniz to carry on his correspondence with Bossuet and the French Jesuits on religious problems.

In the same way, the conflicting ideologies of the nineteenth century all shared the common intellectual background of the European Enlightenment. All of them possessed a similar faith in social and scientific progress. All of them were liberal in the sense that they believed in the

Rights of Man and regarded individual liberty, national freedom or social equality as the supreme good. Marx and Mazzini, Blanqui and Bakunin, Proudhon and Louis Blanc were all children of the Revolution and their internecine feuds were like those of the Jacobins and the Girondins in the days of the First Republic.

At the same time, the breach between the ideologies and Christianity was neither complete nor consistent at this period. Between 1830 and 1850 a certain *rapprochement* between them took place, and Liberals like Lamartine, Socialists like Bazard and Democrats like Leroux claimed that their ideas represented a new application of Christian principles to the political and economic spheres. This was especially the case in Great Britain, where the ideologies possessed no revolutionary background. Here Liberalism owed its political influence to its alliance with the Nonconformist Churches, and the Labour movement developed under the leadership of pious Nonconformists and lay preachers like Burt, Fenwick and Keir Hardie. This is not surprising when one remembers that in Great Britain the connection between political opposition and religious dissent dates back to the Puritan revolution of the seventeenth century and that this tradition has never been entirely lost.

This is a tradition which England shares with America, in contrast to the Continent, since the American Revolution, in spite of its close connection with the European Enlightenment, also owed much to the Puritan tradition, which had survived almost intact in New England. In Russia, on the other hand, where the new Western ideologies did not penetrate until the nineteenth century, the opposition between them and the traditional culture of Orthodox Christendom was from the beginning conscious and avowed and this is one of the chief causes that has led to that polar opposition between Russian Communism and American Democracy which now divides the world.

Thus it would seem that the political and ideological disunity of Europe in the past has been a source of strength, as well as of weakness, since in spite of the heavy cost which this disunity has involved, it has given Europe the opportunity of developing a richer and more many-sided pattern of life and thought than could have been achieved by a more unitary type of culture.

Moreover, this tradition of diversity does not date from the Reformation and the religious divisions of Western Christendom, although it was accentuated by them. Its origins are much earlier, and it represents something that is inseparable from the nature of European culture. The origins of Europe as a civilization are due not only to the extension of the higher culture of the old Mediterranean world to Western and Northern Europe, but also to the dual character of this cultural inheritance. For the culture of the Later Roman Empire, which was handed on to the Latin West and the Byzantine East, was compounded of two elements: the classical culture of Greece and Rome and the religious culture of the Christian Church. Each of these elements possessed its own moral and intellectual traditions, which were embodied in different literatures, different social institutions and different ethical systems.

At first glance it seems as though the fall of the Empire must have involved the disappearance of the classical tradition, since the Church remained the only link between the barbarian peoples and the civilization of the ancient world; and the monasteries, which were the chief centres of literary culture, were devoted by their institution to the ascetic ideals that seemed most irreconcilable with the spirit of classical humanism. In fact, however, it was the monasteries that secured the survival of the inheritance of classical culture through their adaptation of the old liberal education of the schools of the Later Roman Empire to the needs of the new ecclesiastical culture. This preservation of the old curriculum of the Liberal Arts meant that classical literature remained the basis of Western intellectual training. Virgil and Cicero, Ovid and Seneca, Horace and Quintilian were not merely school books, they became the seeds of a new growth of classical humanism in Western soil. Again and again—in the eighth century as well as in the twelfth and fifteenth centuries—the higher culture of Western Europe was fertilized by renewed contacts with the literary sources of classical culture. At first this influence only reached a small clerical minority, but it steadily increased throughout the later Middle Ages until, by the time of the Renaissance, it became the basis of lay education and inspired the development of vernacular literatures.

In this way the tradition of classical culture, which is also the tradition of humanism, became one of the great formative elements in Western culture. But this did not involve the denial or supersession of the Christian tradition, as has often been suggested by the historians of the Renaissance or the Enlightenment. As the humanist tradition remained alive during the Middle Ages, so the Christian tradition preserved its vitality in the post-Renaissance period, and it is only when both these traditions remain in living and fruitful contact with one another that Western culture attains its highest and most characteristic achievements. Nevertheless, this harmony and sympathetic collaboration between two such diverse traditions is difficult to maintain, and their diversity and tension have manifested themselves throughout the course of European history in those religious and ideological conflicts which I have already discussed. The unity of Europe has always been much more fragile than that of the great civilizations of Asia but at the same time it has been more flexible and more capable than any other culture of assimilating new elements and producing new movements of thought and new forms of social institutions.

Seen from this point of view, the modern ideologies are characteristic products of European culture. They become a symptom of cultural decadence only when they become totalitarian and attempt to destroy the spiritual foundations on which European culture is based. Christianity and humanism are both super-ideological in character. They create ideologies, but are not created by them. Their origins are older than those of Europe itself and they extend their influence far into the unconscious depths of the soul of Western man.

Hence the attempt to confine the whole of Western civilization in the strait-jacket of an ideology and to exclude all cultural and spiritual values which are not created by it or dependent on it is destructive of the inner nature of Western culture and must inevitably lead to disaster.

No doubt the Communist will argue that this is a necessary stage in the evolution of modern culture; that as the feudal Christian order was replaced by the bourgeois humanist order, so the latter must now give place to the new social order of scientific social ideology based on modern science. But if science is divorced from humanism and Christianity, it ceases to be a creative source of culture. It is capable of creating new scientific techniques and technologies but these are the servants of the dominant ideology which, in its turn, is the servant of a political party or dictator. No civilization can live by politics alone, and when a culture becomes merely an organ of political propaganda it is dead.

At the present time the existence of Europe is threatened, first by the ideologies which sprang originally from the revolutionary idealism of the Western mind and its boundless faith in social progress, and secondly by the scientific technologies which were invented to serve the cause of life and which have been perverted to the service of destruction. But this is no longer a purely European problem; it has become a world-wide issue. If the ideological division of the world becomes permanent and complete, and if the new world powers employ all the resources of science and technology in the attempt to destroy one another, it is difficult to see how any civilization can survive anywhere. No doubt Europe would be the first to suffer, but the destruction of Europe would only be the prelude to the destruction of the world.

If, on the other hand, humanity decides not to commit suicide, and the new world powers achieve some kind of modus vivendi or balance of power which makes it possible for them to exist together, as the opposing religious forces in Western Europe managed to coexist after the wars of religion, then Europe will still hold a key position in the development of world culture. For Europe is the only cultural area in which all the ideologies meet, and it is the only culture which still maintains a living contact with the deeper spiritual traditions which underlie and transcend the ideologies.

The creators of the modern ideologies—Marx and Mazzini, John Stuart Mill and Herbert Spencer, Saint-Simon and Comte, Herzen and Proudhon—were all members of the same European society who shared a common background of Western humanist culture, whereas their spiritual descendants and heirs have spread abroad to the four corners of the world, where they are becoming progressively alienated from one another by the influence of the different cultural and racial environments with which they have been identified. Consequently it is in Europe, rather than in Asia or the Antipodes, that the criticism and revision of the ideologies can best be carried out and where they can be made intelligible to one another.

But this is possible only if Western culture retains its vital contact with the two great traditions of Christianity and humanism to which it owes its spiritual existence and its unique world-changing character. The survival of these traditions is far more important than that of European political and economic power, just as the survival of Hellenism was more important than that of the Roman Empire. Consequently, the greatest danger that threatens us is not the external threat to our political independence by the expansion of the new world empires, but the internal disintegration of Western culture by the ideologies which are anti-Christian or anti-humanist.

The fact that these ideologies have become completely identified with political parties, social regimes and military alliances makes them far more impervious to intellectual criticism than they were in their earlier formative phase. On the other hand, the same process which has increased their power has also diminished their spiritual appeal. When the ideologies represented the inner conviction and ideals of a revolutionary intelligentsia or a reformist elite, they aroused a similar psychological response to that of a religious sect. But now that they have become the dogmas of a police state, they have become part of the political organization that they serve.

Now if this situation is clearly recognized in Europe and if Western man agrees to confine the ideologies to their proper sphere and to treat them as alternative programmes of social reform and political action, there is no reason why they should be irreconcilable with the traditions of Western culture. The danger comes from their invasion of the world of religion and metaphysics, so that they claim man's spiritual allegiance even in "the things that are not Caesar's." And they have succeeded in doing so because the spiritual tradition of Western culture had been undermined by that spirit of European nihilism which Nietzsche saw with such tragic intensity in the last century. This nihilism is a peculiarly European disease, a malady of the Western spirit which has extended its influence not only to Russia but also to America. Indeed, nowhere has it found clearer expression than in the writings of a modern American poet like Robinson Jeffers.

This particular development is very closely connected

with the ideologies themselves and is a symptom not, as Nietzsche believed, of the mortal sickness of Christianity and humanism, but rather of the exhaustion of the revolutionary tradition itself. Neither Christianity nor humanism is dead. They still possess an infinite capacity of spiritual regeneration and cultural renaissance. What is passing away is the utopian idealism which was the original inspiration of all the revolutionary ideologies. Now that they have been brought down from the clouds to solid earth they have gained temporal power, but they have lost their old appeal. In so far as they continue to press their total claim to man's spiritual allegiance, they must inevitably drive civilization further and further toward nihilism and self-destruction.

The vital task for Europe at the present time is to resist this tendency and to recover and fortify the two great spiritual traditions which are the roots of its culture. This is a difficult task, and one which cannot be achieved without great moral and intellectual efforts. But it is by no means an impossible task, and since Europe was the original creator of the ideologies, she has a special responsibility and a special opportunity for finding a solution to the problems which the ideologies have raised.

ASIA AND THE WEST

6

Introduction: The Revolt of Asia

THE revolt of Asia is not simply an insurrection against alien domination and the influence of foreign ideas. It is also—and even more—a political and moral revolution in the internal order of the oriental peoples. During the last generation, the oldest and the most fundamental institutions which seemed to be inseparable from Asiatic civilization have lost their sacred prestige and are threatened with change or destruction.

What we are witnessing is, in fact, the extension to Asia and to the whole world of the revolutionary movement of change which started in Western Europe and America in the eighteenth century. As that movement began within the limits of the privileged aristocratic class and was transmitted first to the European *bourgeoisie* and then to the proletariat, so it has spread from the dominant nations of Western Europe—first to Eastern Europe and then to the peoples of Asia and Africa.

Therefore Western man has to shoulder a double responsibility. He is the archetypal revolutionary—the Prometheus who stole fire from heaven and set the world ablaze. Yet at the same time he is an imperialist, a capitalist and an exploiter—the obvious target for the criticism and moral indignation of the old peoples of Asia and the new peoples of Africa whom he has both awakened and enslaved.

This is an awkward and confusing situation for both parties, and we cannot be surprised that the relations between Europe and Asia should be marked by mutual resentment and misunderstanding. The men who come to the top in revolutionary movements are never the wisest or the most farsighted of men. On the contrary, revolutions provide an opportunity for the crank, the fanatic and the power maniac, so that a movement which is inaugurated in a mood of boundless optimism and generous idealism soon degenerates into a merciless war of factions and leads through massacre and persecution to some new form of tyranny.

And a similar process takes place in the sphere of ideology. In the war of ideas, it is the crudest and the most simplified ideology that wins. During our own lifetimes we have seen spectacular examples of this. We have seen great and highly civilized countries becoming infected by epidemics of ideological insanity, and whole populations being destroyed for the sake of some irrational slogan.

In the case of Asia, the situation is fortunately less acute. The very immensity of the crisis and the fact that the revolution is long drawn out and spread over many different areas allows us a certain breathing space and an opportunity to readjust our ideas. At the present time it is difficult to detach ourselves and view the problem as a whole. For the politician and the economist are so immersed in the day-to-day course of the struggle that they cannot look beyond its immediate effects on their particular society, while the philosopher and the man of letters are apt to be so appalled by the irrationality of the conflicting forces that they avert their eyes to their abstract or private worlds. But for the Christian neither of these alternatives is possible. He is committed not merely by the fact that he shares in the common responsibility of Western men, but because he is obliged to look beyond the political and economic conflicts of the present time to the ultimate spiritual issues on which the fate of the human race depends. For the Christian, no less than the Marxian, has an historical point of view and knows, however obscurely, the goal towards which the world is moving. This view depends on the doctrine of Divine Providence. Whatever else is obscure, it is certain that God is the governor of the universe and behind the apparent disorder and confusion of history there is the creative action of the divine law. Man is a free agent and is continually attempting to shape the world and the course of history to his own designs and interests. But behind the weak power and the blind science of man, there is the overruling purpose of God which uses man and his kingdoms and empires for ends of which he knows nothing and which are often the opposite of those which man desires and seeks to attain.

It may be objected that a theodicy of this kind is of little practical value. If history is carrying man to an unknown goal in obedience to an inscrutable power, there is nothing man can do about it. But the Christian view of history is not just a blind fatalism. It also asserts the principle of divine revelation and admits the possibility of human cooperation with the divine purpose. No doubt man has to work in the dark, for it is the condition of Christian existence to live by faith and not by sight. Nevertheless, there are moments when the obscurity of history seems to be suddenly illuminated by some sign of divine purpose. These are the moments of *crisis* in the literal sense of the word—times of judgment when the powers of this world are tried and condemned and when the course of history suddenly flows into a new channel. Such was the age of the Hebrew prophets, such was the age of St. Augustine, and such is the age in which we have the privilege and the misfortune to live today. For the present century has been an apocalyptic age —a time of judgment in which the established powers and authorities of the world have been put through the fire and destroyed or renewed, and when civilizations that have endured for thousands of years are being forced into a new mould.

The most important factor in this process, both as cause and result, is the increasing tendency to world unity. It had its origins centuries ago in the Age of Discovery, when the Western mariners opened the new oceanic highways and demonstrated in practice what they had long known in theory—that the world was round and that there were no barriers that could not be surmounted by courage and ingenuity. Thereafter, century by century Western men extended this trade and navigation, until East and West were drawn closer and closer together by a vast intercontinental network of trade and communication.

During the present century this process attained its climax. The world was brought even closer together by the triumphs of Western science and technology. There was a vast expansion of world population and wealth and a related increase of knowledge and communication.

But these changes have also had a revolutionary effect on politics and culture. In the last fifty years all the historic empires that ruled Asia have fallen, and a multitude of new states and nations have emerged out of the ruins. All these new powers are animated by hostility to Western hegemony and an intense desire to assert their national independence. But at the same time, they are not opposed to the new cosmopolitan civilization which was the fruit of the Western expansion. It is rather that they wish to be active partners in it and to appropriate their full share in the material benefits that it has brought. They are in revolt not merely against the West, but against their own past—against the whole traditional order of the old oriental cultures in which the whole of man's life from the cradle to the grave was bound by custom and precedent, enforced by the sanctions of a sacred law. This twofold revolution is the source of our present problems. The peoples of Asia have been forced against their will into a new cosmopolitan society which is predominantly Western in its principles and values, and at the same time they are reacting violently in defence of their national being. This reaction, however, is not directed against the new world order itself, but against the external powers that gave them a subordinate place in it. This nationalist reaction may easily become reactionary or destructive. In extreme cases, especially in Africa, it may lead to a reaction against civilization itself, and a return to pagan barbarism. But in principle it represents the natural and legitimate protest of societies which have been torn from their old moorings and plunged into a storm of change. Unfortunately the peoples of Asia and Africa have not only to cope with the inherent difficulties of the modern revolution —the sudden change from the pace of the ox to that of the aeroplane; they are being forced to make the change under the aegis of a new form of political organization—the sovereign nation state—which has no roots in their own past. The ancient civilizations of Asia had created their own institutions and social hierarchies, which made it possible for peoples of different languages and religion to follow their own laws and customs without interfering with one another, and this system was often maintained by the Western colonial or imperial powers, notably by the British in India. But the coming of nationalism and the modern nation state has destroyed this traditional modus vivendi and has forced the racial and religious minorities to conform themselves to a common pattern.

Hence the new order in Asia is full of explosive possibilities. Nationalism has nowhere been a force that makes for peace, and the new oriental nationalisms are exceptionally aggressive and intolerant. Nevertheless what they need above all else is peace—internal peace to solve the manifold problems of their new existence, and external peace to avoid a cataclysm which would destroy all the gains of the last half century. The danger of such a catastrophe was never greater than it is today when the Asiatic scene is overshadowed by the cold war between two giant world powers with their rival ideologies and economic systems. But there is still room for the intervention of another factor of a different order. In the past religion has been the greatest of the powers that formed the mind and developed the cultures of the Asiatic peoples. At the present moment it is in eclipse owing to the wave of secular influences that has accompanied the spread of Western culture. But it is too soon to say how far this eclipse will go. Certainly it is not total and there seems little probability that it will ever become so.

This is the most important aspect of the whole oriental problem, and it demands much fuller study than it has yet received. When one considers the amount of study that is being devoted to the purely political aspects of oriental nationalism, Christians cannot but feel ashamed of the little that has been done towards the understanding of the new religious situation arising from the revolutionary changes of the last fifty years. Neither the technological process that is forcing East and West together nor the insurgence of the nationalist forces that is tearing them apart can save the modern world from destruction. Salvation can only come from some power capable of creating a spiritual unity which will transcend and comprehend the material unity of the new world order. And where can this power be found save in religion?

7

The Age of Discovery[1]

THE change in the world position of Europe which has taken place during the last fifty years has inevitably caused a strong reaction against the spirit of nineteenth-century imperialism. The idea of empire has become identified with the oppression of subject peoples, and the whole colonial development is regarded as a form of economic exploitation. Yet the imperialist phase of Western culture is not confined to the second half of the nineteenth century. It was the culmination of a much wider movement which goes back to the close of the Middle Ages and which has been one of the main forces in the formation of the modern world. However great may be our moral disapproval of *Homo Europaeus* in his relations with weaker and more primitive peoples, we cannot ignore his positive achievements, for they have changed the face of the earth and created a new world, or even a number of new worlds. Consequently it is impossible to understand the nature of the present world crisis apart from the Western movement of colonial expansion which has transformed the closed Mediterranean continental world

[1] This chapter contains brief excerpts from *Understanding Europe* (New York, 1952), *Religion and the Rise of Western Culture* (New York, 1950), and *The Judgment of the Nations* (New York, 1942).

106

of ancient and medieval culture into an oceanic civilization which has unified the world.

As I wrote concerning the nature of that process ten years ago: "How did it come about that a small group of peoples in Western Europe should in a relatively short space of time acquire the power to transform the world and to emancipate themselves from man's age-long dependence on the forces of nature? In the past this miraculous achievement was explained as the manifestation of a universal Law of Progress which governed the universe and led mankind by inevitable stages from apehood to perfection. Today such theories are no longer acceptable, since we have come to see how much they depend on an irrational optimism which was part of the phenomenon they attempted to explain. Instead we now tend to ask ourselves what were the factors in European culture which explain the peculiar achievement of Western man? or to use the brutal and expressive American phrase, 'What makes him tick?' But when we reach this point we shall find the religious factor does have a very important bearing upon the question.

"For, side by side with the natural aggressiveness and the lust for power which are so evident in European history, there were also new spiritual forces driving Western man towards a new destiny. The activity of the Western mind, which manifested itself alike in scientific and technical invention as well as in geographical discovery, was not the natural inheritance of a particular biological type; it was the result of a long process of education which gradually changed the orientation of human thought and enlarged the possibilities of social action.

"The other great world cultures realized their own synthesis between religion and life and then maintained their sacred order unchanged for centuries and millennia. But Western civilization has been the great ferment of change in the world, because the changing of the world became an integral part of its cultural ideal."[2]

There is no doubt, however, that the rapid material progress and external expansion of Western culture has coincided with its increasing secularization, so that the religious element seems less prominent in the very period when the influence of Western civilization has been most widespread, and this in turn has meant the spread of a secularized culture throughout the world. Now it is true that world empires usually tend to lose touch with their spiritual roots, and the same factor may be seen at work in the expansion of a civilization by way of administrative and intellectual influence, as in the Hellenistic world culture in the third and second centuries B.C. However, this is not the basic cause for the process of secularization which has occurred. For Western culture was becoming secularized before the great period of its expansion had begun. The fundamental causes of that process were spiritual and closely related to the whole spiritual development of Western Man. But the same causes which produced the secularization of culture were also responsible for its external expansion. They were, in fact, two aspects of a single process, a world revolution of such a tremendous kind that it seems to transcend history and create new categories with which our traditional standards of judgment are incapable of dealing.

It is with regard to the religious issue that the traditional

[2] *Religion and the Rise of Western Culture,* pp. 8, 10.

methods of interpretation are most defective. For if we consider the problem from a Christian point of view we are faced by the paradox that it was a Christian culture and not a pagan one which was the source of this revolution. While the secular historian is brought up against the equally disturbing fact that the non-secular element in Western culture has been the dynamic element in the whole process of change, so that the complete secularization of culture by removing this element would bring the progressive movement to a full stop, and thus bring about a static society which has mastered social change to such a degree that it no longer possesses any vital momentum.

Nevertheless the new lay humanist culture which was beginning to develop in the West in the fifteenth and sixteenth centuries was far from being entirely secular. As Burdach has shown, the very conception of the Renaissance—or the rebirth of culture—was closely connected with the Reformation or the rebirth of Christianity. Both were influenced in their origins by the apocalyptic hopes of a spiritual renewal of Christendom, which was so widespread in the later Middle Ages and which found different forms of expression in Northern and Southern Europe. Neither the Humanists nor the Reformers dreamt of the destruction of Christendom. They believed, like Erasmus, that "the world was coming to its senses as if awakening out of a deep sleep," and they thought that religion and culture could slough off their old skins and could renew their youth by returning to their origins.

Thus the Renaissance achievement was like that of Columbus, who discovered the new world by attempting to find his way back to the old world by a new route. The sudden removal of the fixed limits which had bounded the thought and action of medieval man, the opening of new worlds and the realization of the boundless possibilities of human reason caused a release of energies which gave Western culture a new world-embracing character. Though Western science was still in its infancy, men like Leonardo da Vinci and Paracelsus and Campanella and Bacon had already begun to realize its world-transforming possibilities:

Glory to Him who knows and can do all [writes Campanella]:

O my art, grandchild to the Primal Wisdom, give something of his fair image which is called Man.

A second God, the First's own miracle, he commands the depths; he mounts to Heaven without wings and counts its motions and measures and its natures.

The wind and the sea he has mastered and the earthly globe with pooped ship he encircles, conquers and beholds, barters and makes his prey.

He sets laws like a God. In his craft, he has given to silent parchment and to paper the power of speech and to distinguish time he gives tongue to brass.

The author of these verses is a striking example of the way in which the thought of the Renaissance united humanist and scientific culture with apocalyptic religious ideals and revolutionary hopes for a new order of society.

Despite the frustration of the idealistic hopes of the Renaissance for the creation of a new social order, in one respect the age of the Renaissance gave birth to a practical result of incalculable importance, which altered the whole future of the world. This was the great movement of navigation and discovery, which at last broke the bounds of the old Mediterranean world and opened the new ocean routes to America and the East. And although these discoveries had a disastrous effect on the commercial prosperity of Italy, it was Italian enterprise above all that rendered them possible. The trading states of Italy were the schools of medieval navigation. They developed the new types of ocean-going ships, and introduced from the Moslem East, as early as the twelfth century, the magnet, as well as the use of the astrolabe and the timepiece without which scientific navigation was impossible. Moreover, it was the Venetians, Marco Polo and his uncles, who first reached China and circumnavigated Asia from Zeitun to the Persian Gulf in the latter part of the thirteenth century and fired the imagination of Europe with their tales of the boundless wealth and population of the East.

The initiation of the great period of discovery was due above all, however, to the vision and tenacity of one man, the Portuguese Prince Henry, afterwards known as the Navigator, who, for more than forty years, from his palace observatory of Sagres on the "Sacred Cape" of Saint Vincent sent out expedition after expedition down the West African coast. He was not a man of the Renaissance, but a pious and ascetic prince after the medieval fashion, who aimed, above all, at gaining a new world for Christendom to compensate for what had been lost to the infidel in the Levant. But he made full use of Italian science and Italian enterprise, and some of his most able captains, like the Venetian Cadamosto, were of Italian origin. And so too in later years it was Italians like the Cabots, and Amerigo Vespucci, Verrazano and, above all, Columbus himself, who were the great pioneers of exploration in the service of the Western powers. The discovery of America by Columbus, and of the Cape route to India by the Portuguese had an immediate and profound effect upon European history. Not only did it revolutionize the trade routes of the old world, it destroyed the age-long eastbound orientation of European culture. The effect on Renaissance Italy was especially important. For three centuries Italy had dominated the Eastern Mediterranean. The prosperity of Genoa was derived from the trade with the Black Sea and that of Venice from that with India by way of Egypt. For a thousand years Italy had been in contact with the Byzantine culture, and in the fifteenth century this influence was stronger than ever owing to the presence of Byzantine scholars like Bessarion and George of Trebizond.

Now, almost simultaneously, her control of the Aegean was threatened by the Turkish conquest, and her monopoly of the oriental trade was destroyed by the new discoveries. The Atlantic ports of Lisbon and Cadiz and Antwerp took the place of Venice and Genoa as the great marts of foreign wares. The Mediterranean, which had been the highway of trade and culture since prehistoric times, suddenly became a backwater.

At the same time, with the conquest of Egypt in 1517 and of Hungary from 1520 to 1530, the whole of the Eastern world from the Danube to the Red Sea was united under the Turkish power, which was far more hostile and dangerous to European culture than the Sultanate of Egypt had ever been.

These changes affected the trade of Venice with extraordinary swiftness. By the year 1509 the Egyptian trade had declined to vanishing point. Nevertheless she held the fragments of her Aegean empire, Cyprus until 1571, Crete until 1669, and preserved some prosperity, as did the rest of North Italy, by industry and trade with Northern Europe. But to these economic catastrophes was added the disaster of foreign invasions and the French and Spanish conquests, which finally put an end to the great age of Italian civilization.

The change of conditions was slower in affecting the Southern German trading cities. In fact, at the beginning of the sixteenth century, their prosperity was at its height and the great capitalist houses of the Fugger and the Welser occupied the same position of international importance that the Florentine bankers had held a century earlier. The towns of Southern Germany, above all Nuremberg and Augsburg, and those of the Rhineland were the scene of a short-lived German Renaissance. It was here that the new arts of printing and engraving were developed—scientists like Peuerbach and Regiomontanus, artists like Dürer and Cranach, scholars like Erasmus of Rotterdam and Reuchlin, rivalled their Italian contemporaries. Nevertheless, the centre of gravity had been moved Westward, and it was the Atlantic powers, Spain, France, England and the Netherlands, that were to dominate the following age, both economically and politically.

The motives which inspired this movement of exploration and discovery which shifted the axis of world power from the Mediterranean to the Atlantic were mixed in character. First there was the religious motive, the continuance of the medieval crusading ideal, which is especially clear in the work of Prince Henry, the great precursor of the Age of Discovery, who conceived the idea of turning the flank of the Moslem world power by the exploration of West Africa and the establishment of a new Christian dominion in Guinea. Nor was it an accident that the discovery of America by Spain was the immediate sequel to the capture of Granada, which ended the long history of the Spanish Reconquest. But from the first the commercial motive also played a great part, especially in the Italian maritime states which had suffered most from the closing of the old trade routes to the East. Yet this economic motive had also existed in the early crusading movement, so far as the participation of the Italian states was concerned. But in the case of Spain, and to a lesser degree of Portugal and France, an attempt was made to subordinate the purely economic factor to the old crusading ideal. The Spanish conquest of America and the French settlement of Quebec and Montreal were thoroughly medieval in spirit. It was the aim of the Spanish government to create a new Christendom across the seas, and the search for gold and land was accompanied by a no less genuine missionary enthusiasm. This motive led the Crown to interpose between the greed of the colonists and the native populations. It inspired the career of Las Casas and the enlightened Indian legislation of the Spanish government, which, however imperfectly carried out, at least saved the native population from extinction. Its most remarkable expression, however, was in the mission states, notably that of the Jesuits in Paraguay, and later that of the Franciscans in California, which forms a unique chapter in colonial history.

The spirit of the Dutch colonial enterprise, on the other hand, is completely different. To them above all is due the creation of a purely economic colonial policy. They came as traders, not as conquerors, still less as missionaries, and their possessions were administered entirely with a view to the interests of the shareholders in the great colonial joint-stock companies, such as the East India Company. The Dutch were the great pioneers of the new colonial and commercial system; and the English, and, from the time of Colbert, the French also, followed in their footsteps. But while the English adopted the Dutch system of commercial colonization and colonial companies, they differed from the Dutch in the predominantly agricultural character of their American colonies; and the consequent growth of a large homogeneous agricultural population across the Atlantic was to have a vast importance for the future development of civilization in the new world.

In addition to the religious and economic factors behind the movement of exploration and colonization, one cannot exclude the influence of two other motives—scientific curiosity and the love of travel, navigation and adventure for their own sakes. Now all these four motives also operated in the case of the Islamic expansion, and the West was thus following in the steps of the earlier oriental movement. To some extent the two movements were contemporaneous, since the Portuguese and Dutch colonization of the East Indies took place at the same period that Mohammedan traders and missionaries were advancing in Indonesia and conquering the older Hindu cultures that had dominated the regime.

For all that, the European expansion had a new and revo-

lutionary character that distinguished it from all that had
gone before. In the course of a single generation—between
1486 and 1536—the world was suddenly transformed by a
series of voyages and discoveries—the circumnavigation of
Africa, the discovery of America, the discovery of India and
the Far East for Western trade, the circumnavigation of the
world, and the conquest of Mexico and Peru. All this represents an extraordinary explosion of human energy, for
none of their results were achieved without hazards of navigation and disease—above all scurvy. (Of Magellan's five
ships only one returned, and of the 270 or 280 men only
35; nor was this an exceptionally bad record.)

In the case of Portugal, it is at first sight difficult to explain how these small expeditions of small ships from one
of the smallest of European states should have been able to
establish a colonial empire throughout the East, from East
Africa to Malaya and Indonesia, in the face of organized
opposition from Egypt and the commercial states of Western India and Indonesia. For these powers possessed all the
advantages of fighting on their own ground, close to their
own bases and supported by the religious sympathies of the
local populations. The phenomenon is undoubtedly a complex one which involves many factors of diverse origin and
value. But beyond all the temporary and accidental factors
the Age of Discovery also seems to represent the energies
of a new type of man and a new attitude to the world which
was to remain characteristic of this new phase of Western
culture. This new type was the product of the impact of
humanism on Christian culture and their combined influence
on the material expansion of the Western European nations,
whose superabundant energies, like those of the Turks and

Mongols, may perhaps be explained biologically as a result of the pressure of population on territory and food supply. (And this last factor may explain why the smallest countries, like Portugal, England and the Netherlands, played such a leading part in the development.) In the Middle Ages, both in the East and the West, there was no lack of interest in travel and exploration and economic enterprise, as we see from the records of the Moslem and Christian travellers like Ibn Batuta and Marco Polo, but there was at the same time a certain moral disapproval and feeling that there was something impious in exceeding the bounds that had been set out by God and Nature on human achievement. We find a popular expression of this in the *Arabian Nights,* where Sindbad, who is inspired by a spirit of enterprise and adventure like an Elizabethan's, feels compelled to apologize for his adventurousness as morally wrong—"My wicked soul suggested to me to travel again to the countries of other people and I felt a longing for associating with the different races of men and for selling and gains."

Even more remarkable is Dante's passage on the last voyage of Ulysses, which seems to express prophetically the new ideal that was to inspire Western man. "O brothers who through a hundred thousand perils have reached the West, do not grudge to the brief space of consciousness that remains to gain experience beyond the sun of the uninhabited world. Consider your origin. You were not made to live like animals, but to seek virtue and knowledge." Yet Dante does not approve of this heroism. He speaks of it as "a mad voyage" and suggests that the fate of the explorers was a just retribution for their folly.

With the Renaissance, the public opinion changed and

the humanists from Politian onwards regard the discoveries in the spirit of Dante's Ulysses. Yet the great poet of the movement, Camoëns, who himself spent most of his life in India and the Moluccas and China in the course of Western expansion and who represents better than any other writer the union of the crusading spirit and the humanist ideal, also gives expression to the traditional medieval feeling in the long speech of the old man of Lisbon at the end of Canto 4, protesting against the false ideals that inspired the colonial movement. "This folly which describes as enterprise and valour what is but the cruel ferocity of the brute creation and boasts of its contempt of life which should always be held dear."[2]

In fact one of the remarkable features of the new European movement is the way in which it has always been accompanied by a spirit of criticism and self-questioning—indeed it is one of the sources of the self-questioning of Western man. Thus the conquest of America led to the Christian humanitarian propaganda of Las Casas—the first of the long series of protests against colonial and imperialist exploitation and of the defence of the rights of native peoples; and in the same way the oriental expansion was accompanied by a tendency towards the appreciation of the value of the oriental cultures. This dualism is the inevitable result of the internal contradictions of European expansion—on the one hand, the economic desire for trade and gold and the exploitation of the new lands, and on the other the missionary call to spread the faith and the Kingdom of God.

[2] From W. C. Atkinson's translation of the *Luciads,* p. 120. (Penguin Classics.)

As I have said, both these motives were already present in the crusading movement, and one recalls the utterances of Franciscan reformers like Roger Bacon and Ramon Lull, who complain that the spiritual purposes of the crusade were stultified by the greed and oppression of the representatives of Christendom. But after the Age of Discovery the contradiction was more glaring, and by the seventeenth century the two aspects of the movement become increasingly divergent and express themselves through different channels.

One, the economic movement, finds its appropriate organ in the great trading companies, above all the Dutch East India Company, which embodied the economic motive in its most marked and ruthless form, especially under the leadership of the great organizer and builder of Dutch rule in Indonesia, Jan Pieterzoon Coen (1586–1627). In the same way the missionary movement was embodied in the religious orders, especially the Jesuits, whose members were often drawn from peoples like the Italians who were not politically involved in the movement of colonial expansion and who did their best to assimilate themselves to their non-European environment. Nevertheless the dominant tendency throughout this whole period was to maintain a close bond between economic, political and religious expansion. This was the policy of Spain in America and the Philippines, of Portugal in Africa and Asia, and of France in Canada, and it was responsible for the destruction of the great work of the Portuguese mission in Japan and Indonesia and ultimately for the decline of the Jesuit mission in China.

It must be emphasized that throughout this period the West had made no impression on the power centres of the oriental world. The great Asiatic empires—Turkey, Persia, the Mogul Empire of Hindustan and China—remained intact; even Japan and Abyssinia were strong enough to exclude Western influence, though this was represented as yet only by missionaries who did not attempt political domination. On the other hand, the West had obtained almost complete mastery of the seas and of maritime trade, and it had conquered the New World of America which was to take an increasingly important part in the balance of world power. This Empire of the Seas was accompanied by an immense growth of scientific knowledge and a technological advance in shipbuilding, navigation and cartography, which laid the foundations of the European world hegemony of the following age.

8

The Fall of the Oriental Empires

DURING the eighteenth and nineteenth centuries, the influence of Western culture began to penetrate the inner continental areas of Asia and Africa, and the historic oriental empires underwent a rapid decline. The first step in this process was the Europeanization of Russia, which had remained for centuries a kind of intermediate zone between Europe and Asia. In the seventeenth century Russian power had expanded rapidly across northern Asia, reaching Okhotsk on the Pacific before the middle of the century, but Russia itself remained outside the sphere of Western culture. It was the revolutionary work of Peter the Great from 1689 to 1725 that forced Russia against its will to become part of Europe. The process was primarily military, secondly technological and industrial, thirdly educational and scientific and fourthly social and artistic. None of these aspects was neglected by Peter, but it was his insistence on the importance of technological change that distinguishes him from his contemporaries and most of his successors. On the other hand the violence and oppressiveness with which he enforced his reforms caused a permanent trauma in mod-

ern Russian culture which shows itself in the Russian revolutionary movement. This was the work of the Europeanized
intelligentsia, but it was at the same time a revolt against
Petrine Russia.

While the new Russia was extending a modified form of
Western culture into the heart of Asia, the old colonial powers were increasing their commercial and maritime pressure,
and the decay of the Mogul Empire in continental India created a political vacuum which was filled by the economic
power of the East India Company out of which arose the
British Empire in India. Now for the first time the higher
culture of the East came under direct Western influence,
and though the process of penetration was a very gradual
one, it was a continuous one which eventually transformed
the traditional order of Indian culture. British rule in India
differed in important respects from all the other imperial
and colonial Empires in history—not only from the Roman
and the Spanish Empires, but also from Dutch and French
colonial movements. This was due to the fact that it was an
authoritarian system based on laissez-faire principles. It was
the policy of the East India Company to insert itself into
the political structure of post-Mogul India with as little dis-
turbance as possible of existing social and economic relations. As Wellington once wrote: "The principle of our
occupation of India has been the protection of the property
in land in the hands of the natives; and with a view to the
attainment of this object the positive prohibition of colonization by Europeans and of the purchase of land by Europeans out of the boundaries of the original settlements."
Thus India was a sort of vast native reserve administered by

the Company as the representative of the Mogul empire, to maintain law and order for the benefit of the native population and of course of the Company itself, which held the monopoly of the trade between India and Europe on the one hand, and India and China on the other. On these principles the Company was not concerned with the spread of Western civilization in India. Its rule was *quieta non moveri,* and it looked askance at the activities of Christian missionaries, and any attempt by social reformers to interfere with Indian customs. It assimilated itself to its surroundings, using Persian as its official language and administering the law according to Islamic and Brahmin codes. Change was inevitable, but it did not come from the government but from the force of circumstances.

Thus the Protestant missionaries based themselves on the Danish settlements of Serampore in Bengal and Tranquebar in the South, but though they had entered India by the back door without the Company's permission, it was difficult for the governors, who were themselves Christians, to deport or silence them. In the same way it was impossible to create an efficient administrative and legal system without introducing reforms that were based consciously or unconsciously on Western ideas. Above all some form of higher education for the Company's employees was indispensable, and as early as the time of Warren Hastings this led to the first real cultural contacts between India and Europe. Hastings was himself a student of oriental literature, and sponsored the first translation of the Bhagavad-Gita in 1785. In 1784 the Asiatic Society of Bengal was founded, and in 1792 the Sanskrit College at Benares. But it was the foundation of the

College at Fort William by Lord Wellesley in 1800 that was epoch-making, since it led to the first use of the vernacular languages in education, and this involved the writing of text-books and the creation of a prose literature in Urdu and Hindi. Thus the origins of the new prose literature not only in Urdu and Hindi, but also in Bengali and the other ver-naculars arose out of the demands of the new educational system, which was itself a product of the contact of Euro-pean and Indian culture. A large share in this work was taken by the Protestant missionaries from Serampore, espe-cially Carey and Marshman who became teachers at Fort William College, though that institution remained strictly non-Christian. And missionaries took a similar part in the teaching and printing of the Dravidian vernacular languages of Southern India.

In the course of time, however, there was an increasing demand and need for the study of English, and from the time of Macaulay's famous *Minute on Education* in 1835, it became the policy of the Government to provide a stand-ardized type of secular, higher education in the English language throughout the country, and it was this common education which in the course of a century became the basis of modern Indian nationality. This is fully recognized by the Indian nationalists themselves, such as Sardar Panikkar, who writes as follows: "In the first place the system of higher education in English provided India with a class imbued with social purposes foreign to Hindu thought. The continu-ity and persistence of those purposes achieved the socio-religious revolution on which the life of modern India is based. While British administration did little or nothing to

emancipate the spirit, to extinguish the prejudices, to eradi-
cate the ravages of ignorant custom and pernicious superstition, the New Learning which came to India through its
introduction to the English language on a nation-wide scale
undoubtedly did all this. Indeed it may be argued that the
essential contradiction of the British rule in India lay in this:
the constituted government upheld the validity of customs,
maintained and administered laws which denied the principles of social justice, refused to legislate for changes ur-
gently called for by society, watched with suspicion the
movement of liberal ideas, while the officially sponsored and
subsidized educational system was undermining everything
that the Government sought to uphold. . . . In the educational system the Government created and maintained an
opposition to itself in a place where its own methods were
ineffectual.

"The mining of the ancient fortress of Hindu custom was
a major achievement, for the reason that it was uniformly
spread all over India. Had the new education been through
the vernacular languages, the emphasis of the movement
would have been different from province to province. . . .
There would have been no 'master plan' of change, and instead of the Hindu community being unified, it would have
split into as many units as there are languages in India. . . .
From this development India was saved by the common
medium of education which Macaulay introduced into India.

"In the second place it is a point of major significance in
the evolution of India as a single nation that this uniform
system of education throughout India through a single language produced a like-mindedness on which it was possible

to build. That it gave to India a common language for political thinking and action is of less importance than the creation of this like-mindedness, this community of thought, feeling and ideas which created the Indian nationality."[1]

Thus it is clear that the success of the British policy in India was due to this combination of political conservatism and educational liberalism. If the Government had attempted to carry out a drastic programme of social reform to modernize Indian culture, it would have united the whole population in a vehement resistance to Western influences: if on the other hand it had followed the advice of the orientalists on the educational commission and had supported a purely traditional type of education based on Sanskrit and Persian and Brahui, Indian culture would have remained isolated and unchanged. The result of the dualist policy was to create a native Indian demand for social and political reform which has led (as Sardar Panikkar shows) to the transformation of the traditional Hindu society into something new. But he does not make it sufficiently clear that this result was foreseen and planned by the founders of the system. In his *Minute on Education,* Macaulay compares the situation in India to that in Russia a hundred years earlier, and it is clear that he envisaged not merely a limited educational reform, but a far-reaching process of cultural transformation through the influence of education.

The first fruits of this process were already visible before Macaulay wrote in the work of Ram Mohun Roy, the great Bengali leader who initiated the liberal reform of Indian cul-

[1] *Asia and Western Dominance* by K. M. Panikkar. Reprinted by permission of The John Day Company, publisher.

ture. Thus it preceded the introduction of Western technology, which was slow to come in India and began only with the construction of the Indian railways and telegraph under Lord Dalhousie, 1848–56. On the other hand the missionaries (mainly the Protestant missionaries) played a great part in the movement from the beginning. Not only did they provide teachers and linguists for the new educational system (as at Fort William College), but they were the only people who attempted to provide primary education, and through their schools they produced a far deeper impression than they did by their preaching. Yet their religious propaganda also had an important effect in awakening the Indian mind and producing the criticism and restatement of Hindu doctrine which were expressed in the new reformist movements of the Brahmo Samaj of Ram Mohun Roy and the Arya Samaj of Dayananda Sarasvati.

Now the same process that proved so effective in India also affected China in the following period. Here as in India, the coming of Western influence was primarily the work of the European trader—in fact of the same traders' organization—the East India Company, whose trade was based on the exchange of the two staples—tea and opium. But here the resistance of the Asiatic polity to European infiltration and to Western culture was far stronger and more effective. The mere establishment of diplomatic relations involved two wars. For Chinese culture was such a highly integrated system, so politically centralized and so socially uniform, that it was difficult for Western culture to penetrate it without destroying it. On the other hand the Chinese empire was undergoing a rapid process of decay all through the nineteenth century, just as the Mogul empire in India had done in the eighteenth century. The great Ch'ing emperors of the seventeenth and eighteenth centuries had raised Chinese prestige and also Chinese self-sufficiency to a point which their successors were unable to maintain. The eunuch-ridden court and the tradition-ridden bureaucracy were incapable alike of resisting the pressure of Western commerce and of controlling popular discontent, which exploded in the great popular rising of the T'ai P'ing rebels, who found their inspiration in the new doctrines preached by Western missionaries. If the Western powers had supported the rebels, the Ch'ing dynasty would have come to an end fifty years earlier than it did, and would have been replaced by a native Christian or semi-Christian new order instead of by a Communist one. Instead, the English and the Americans used their influence to support the government in return for the opening of the country to Western traders and missionaries. Gordon helped to suppress the T'ai P'ing, and later Robert Hart reorganized the Chinese customs service with considerable benefit to the national finances. In this, both Gordon and Hart acted as servants of the Chinese empire and formed a temporary buffer between the old system and the pressure of Western powers. At the same time, the missionaries, under the protection of the Western treaties, increased this propaganda and attempted to establish schools and hospitals. It was largely through their influence that during the second half of the nineteenth century some attempt was made by Chinese reformers, like Yung Wing, to acquire Western knowledge and to send students to America and Europe. But these attempts were frustrated by the dead hand of official traditionalism, and by the sinister influence of the Empress and the court eunuchs. It was not until the Japanese war of 1894 that China was forced to face the need for modernization. Even then the party of reform, though supported by the Emperor, was defeated by the Dowager Empress, who for her part supported the anti-foreign reaction of the Boxer Movement. This was the most disastrous mistake ever committed by a responsible government, since it led to the complete defeat and discredit of the Empire, and rendered the Chinese revolution of the twentieth century inevitable.

The history of the penetration of Western culture into Japan offers an extraordinary contrast to the case of China. Japan had excluded Western influence—and especially missionary influence—far more drastically than China for more than 200 years. Yet the acceptance of Western culture in the second half of the nineteenth century was extraordinarily rapid and successful, and it resulted in Japan achieving an international status as a world power which distinguished it from all other non-Western states. What is the explanation of this remarkable achievement?

In the first place Japan was the only country of Asia which accepted the necessity of Westernization with open eyes, and deliberately set herself to control the process of modernization in the interests of the nation as a whole. In the second place, the reform coincided with an internal political revolution which was not due to Western influence, but had the authority and prestige of the sacred monarchy behind it. And thirdly the reforms were carried out by an exceptionally able group of statesmen—Prince Ito, Okubo

Toshimichi, Kido Junichiro, and Goto Shojiro—such as
were not to be found in any other Asiatic country at the
time. The credit for this must be ascribed in some measure
to the old system that they replaced, for the Tokuyawa
regime had instilled into the ruling (Samurai) classes an
exceptionally high standard of social discipline and responsibility. Indeed the moral ideal of the Legacy of Ieyasu ex-
presses a spirit of stern self-repression and moral activism
which has much in common with the Western traditions of
Stoicism and Puritanism. It was this spirit of social discipline
which enabled the reformers to overcome the xenophobia
of the conservative opposition, which was as violent as anything to be found in China or in Islam. In 1858 their leader,
Mito Nariaki, one of the most influential men in Japan, went
so far as to demand that the negotiators of the Treaty with
America should be forced to commit suicide and that the
American minister himself should be decapitated. For a time
anyone who carried an umbrella was liable to be cut down
by swordsmen who resented this badge of foreign barbarism!
Nevertheless in a few years the whole people was induced
to abandon the cherished laws and customs of the past,
to adopt European dress, European laws and a European
constitution.

But these sacrifices were not unrewarded. Population
and wealth increased, and above all, the naval and military
power of Japan advanced with startling rapidity. The war
with China in 1894–5 made her the strongest power in Asia,
and the Russo-Japanese war in 1904–5 showed that she
could meet and defeat one of the greatest military powers of
the West. This war marks a turning point in world history,

since it had widespread repercussions throughout the East and did more than any other single factor to stimulate the new spirit of oriental nationalism.

But the expansion of Western power and culture in the eighteenth and nineteenth centuries was not confined to the East. In many respects it was the Western development which was the most important, for nothing altered the balance of world power and population more decisively than the growth of a new centre of Western culture across the Atlantic. This development was almost entirely the work of the eighteenth and nineteenth centuries. At the beginning of the eighteenth century the colonization of the North American continent had hardly begun, and the English population were confined to a narrow and discontinuous fringe of settlements along the Atlantic coast. But from the Peace of Utrecht (1713), a process of expansion began which continued without a break for two centuries, until the whole continent was occupied from sea to sea. The Revolution and the Civil War were mere episodes by comparison with this vast movement of population. Far more important was the coming of the steamship and the railway which increased the volume of immigration and transformed the movement from a British to a pan-European one, and made North America a crucible in which elements from every European country were fused into a new national unity.

Hence the ambivalence of the American tradition. For the American people became international in its composition without losing its strong sense of nationality and national patriotism; and at the same time, although it owed its existence to colonialism and was in fact the greatest of all the European colonies, it possessed a conscious anti-colonial ethos which leads Americans to sympathize with the peoples of the East (especially perhaps with the Indians and Indonesians) in their resistance to Western (European) influences. In South America and Mexico the pattern of colonialism is very different; there the work of colonization was carried out in the previous periods—and especially the sixteenth century—and it left a large native population in existence, so that the situation in Central America and the Andean republics resembles that of the European colonies in Asia and Africa rather than that of the United States. Only in the Argentine and South Brazil are conditions favourable to a development of the North American type. In the British dominions, on the other hand, in Canada and Australia and New Zealand, the social pattern is similar to that of the U.S.A., although the scale of development has been much smaller and the new societies are less international in composition. Yet they too have contributed to the change in the axis of world power, by the establishment of centres of Western culture in the Pacific and the Antipodes.

To sum up: this period of two centuries saw the irremediable decline of the three great oriental empires owing to their own internal weakness rather than to direct pressure from the West. But the power vacuum thus created was filled by the growth of Western economic and naval and military power. The most important result of this process was not the building of the colonial empires, important as these were, but the creation of a world-wide network of communications and commercial relations based on Western maritime power and on an international system of credit and finance. The banker, the merchant, the consul, the shipper, the engineer, the planter and the colonist formed the links of a continuous chain extending from London and New York to the islands of the Pacific, the rivers of China and the rice fields of India and Burma. The maintenance of this chain involved the charting and policing of the seven seas, the suppression of piracy and the slave trade and the enforcement of Western commercial law in Asiatic communities. It was essentially a cosmopolitan system based on the economic liberalism of Adam Smith and the English economists, and it involved the opening of the world not only to the Western trader, but also to the explorer, the scientist and the missionary. The great age of expansion during the nineteenth century was the golden age of the individual pioneer, naturalists like Darwin and Wallace and Fortune, explorers like Barth and Lander and Caillet, orientalists like Lane and Hodgson and Burton, missionaries like Livingstone and Huc and Judson.

The total impact of the West on the East during this period is incalculable, since it was diffused through a thousand different channels, and the rivalry and competition between the different European powers multiplied the opportunities of infiltration. Only the most remote and thinly peopled regions of the world—Tibet, Arabia and Mongolia —were able to maintain their isolation, and even in these cases the attempt to exclude Western influence stimulated the efforts of Western explorers to break through the curtain. Of course there have always been intrepid travellers in the East as well as the West—Chinese monks in ancient India, Arab merchants in medieval Russia and Africa, et cetera—but it was only in the Western expansion that exploration was literally world-wide and that every drop of knowledge was collected and canalized by academies and learned institutions into one vast river of universal knowledge which fertilized every province of culture.

Nor should the predominantly economic and capitalist character of this movement of Western expansion lead us to ignore its spiritual aspects. The religious, scientific and humanitarian motives and factors in the movement were all of them important.

The remarkable cultural work of the Catholic missionaries in the East continued into the early part of this period. Indeed it was during the eighteenth century that the Jesuits did most to spread the knowledge of Chinese culture and history in Europe. Nevertheless the eighteenth century was a period of decline and even of catastrophe for the Catholic missions. The controversy on the Chinese rites resulted in the formal prohibition of the preaching of Christianity in China. Still more disastrous for the missions, alike in Asia and elsewhere, was the suppression of the Jesuits by the Papacy in 1773, and this was soon followed by the French Revolution, which practically put an end to Catholic missionary activity for a generation. The discouragement and defeatism which was caused by these events finds expression in the "Letters on the State of Christianity in India," which the Abbé Dubois published after his return to Europe in 1823 from a mission that had lasted for thirty years, and in which he regards the conversion of the higher castes of Hinduism as a hopeless task. Nevertheless the nineteenth century saw a remarkable and world-wide revival of missionary activity, so that, as we have seen, the American historian of Christian Missions, Professor Latourette, has entitled it "The Great Century." The new movement, which began in the last decade of the eighteenth century, was Protestant in origin and was especially associated with the pietist sects—Moravian, Baptist and Wesleyan, and with the Evangelical movement in the Church of England. Unlike the earlier Jesuit movement, the new missionaries made no attempt to adapt themselves to oriental culture. In fact they were frankly and naively Western in their approach, denouncing native culture as tainted with heathenism, and advocating Western ideas, Western education and Western trade.[2] It was through their agency that the influence of Western culture first reached the mind of the Eastern peoples. It was not always a very high type of culture, and with some eminent exceptions, it did not reach the most highly educated representatives of oriental culture—the Brahmins, the Confucian scholars and the Arab and Persian "ulama." But it promoted the meeting of East and West on a middle ground, between Europeans and Asiatics who neither of them belonged to the ruling caste in their respective communities. Most of the missionaries were of humble origins. The great pioneer in India, William Carey (1761–1834), who did more than any man of his generation for the study of Indian languages, was a village shoemaker from Northamptonshire, Marshman was the son of a weaver, Morrison (1782–1834), the first Protestant missionary to China, had been a bootmaker. Yet it was these men and others like them who

[2] In this last respect Livingstone's Travels and Journals are very instructive, since he regards the missionary and the trader as allies through whose co-operation alone the slave trade can be suppressed.

did far more than the scholars and the administrators to introduce Western education into the East and to promote the study of oriental languages.

This Protestant missionary movement was followed in the course of the nineteenth century by a great revival of Catholic missions, which was supported by the restoration of the Jesuits and the foundation of new missionary orders, most of them French in origin and recruitment. But on the whole it was the Protestant missionaries, especially in China and India, who had the greatest educational influence, since it was they who identified themselves most completely with Western cultural views. The Catholics concentrated their energies on building strong local Christian communities, while the Protestants favoured broadcast propaganda by preaching, literature and education designed to reach the widest possible public.

This approach was especially important in China, where the missionaries for a long time provided the only access to Western knowledge, as we see from the outstanding case of Sun Yat-sen himself. He received his early education at Bishop's College in Honolulu and at Hong Kong, where he became a Christian. He was afterwards trained as a doctor at the American hospital at Canton, and at the London Missionary Society's medical school at Hong Kong. Thus his whole career was moulded by missionary influences, and it was as a Christian that he began his campaign for the political reform of China on Western democratic lines.

In fact the whole movement of reform in the later nineteenth century, which was the forerunner of the Chinese Revolution, was steeped in missionary influences. The most influential thinker and writer of that movement, Liang Ch'i-Ch'ao, acted for years as the secretary of the Welsh missionary, Timothy Richards, who had many friends among Chinese intellectuals, and exerted great influence in educational matters. And still earlier, an American missionary, W. H. P. Martin, had been appointed head of the Tung Wen Kuan College which had been founded in 1862, to train the candidates for the foreign service. And these are only the most outstanding examples of a large class that included learned sinologists like James Legge and Alexander Wylie, as well as medical missionaries and popularizers of Western science.

Elsewhere in Asia, the influence of the missionaries was not so great, since in Japan the impetus to change came from the government itself, and in India it was the influence of the official system of Western education that was most important. Yet there also the missionaries continued to play an important part alike in the higher education[3] and in popular education. It was the missionaries above all who attacked the fundamental social problem of India—the question of caste—and who were the first to attempt to raise the social and intellectual position of the Untouchables.

But it is obvious that in spite of the agreement between the ideals of the Protestant missionaries, and the liberal gospel of free trade and social progress, there was an obvious contradiction between Christian ideals and the realities of Western commercial exploitation. The conflict was sharpest

[3] It is significant that even today so prominent a Hindu leader as Sardar Panikkar should have received a Christian education—first in a C.M.S. High School, and then at St. Paul's School and at the Madras Christian College.

in the less civilized areas, as in Africa and the Pacific.[4] But it was sufficiently evident in Indonesia, where the tradition of economic exploitation was deeply rooted, and in China, where the Europeans were identified with the opium trade and the coolie traffic. The idea of imperialism is nothing new in Asia, where political oppression has been as inevitable as war and famine and disease. But commercial exploitation and the privileged position of the foreign merchant and money lender is alien to their traditions and arouses a strong moral resistance. The ruthless exploitation of their economic opportunities by the English traders and bankers in India in the eighteenth century and by Western traders in China and elsewhere in the following period did more than anything else to sow the seeds of the anti-Western sentiment which was ultimately to become a dominant factor in the relations of East and West.

[4] There is a good picture of the relations of traders and missionaries drawn from life in R. L. Stevenson's little masterpiece "The Beach of Falesa."

they have got it with a vengeance, and no one can foretell what the results will be.

It is perhaps difficult for us to realize the importance of what is happening. The national state and the concept of nationality have been familiar to us in the West for centuries, but in Asia during the past, nationality and even the State as we know it hardly existed. There was kingship and empire, and the ideal of a universal monarchy had existed ever since the days of the Persian King of Kings and even back to Sargon of Akkad. When the western European nations were acquiring political form the Asian world was dominated by a real world monarchy, the Mongol Empire which ruled from the Pacific to the Black Sea. In later times the oriental world was dominated by three great empires, the Turkish Empire in the Near East, the Mogul Empire in India, and the Chinese Empire in the Far East; but none of these were political societies of the same type as the Western nation states are. They were far removed from the interests and anxieties of the ordinary man, whom one cannot even call a citizen. The most important functions of the modern Western State were performed by other social institutions; by the sub-caste in India, by the family and clan in China and by the tribe or religious community, or *millet,* in the Turkish Empire. Politics was in theory the business of kings and in practice was often an affair of intrigues by the eunuchs of the court or conspiracies by mercenary soldiers. The idea of the ordinary man's having anything to do with politics was unheard of and when the first nationalists in the East tried to make their voices heard they paid for it with their heads. Nothing is more instructive than the terms

of the sentence of death, in 1859, on Yoshida Torajiro or
Shoin, the Japanese nationalist, whose story was told long
ago by R. L. Stevenson. The text of the sentence is as follows:[1]

Item.   He tried to go to America.
Item.   He advised the Government on central defence
        while in jail.
Item.   He opposed the hereditary succession to office
        and favoured the selection of able men by popu-
        lar vote.
Item.   He planned to give his opinion regarding foreign-
        ers to the Bakufu.
Item.   He did such things while in domiciliary confine-
        ment, thus showing great disrespect for high
        officials.

The emergence of the Asiatic peoples from this state of
total subservience to a state of political consciousness, self-
determination and full citizenship has been the great mission
of oriental nationalism and that is why it arouses such intense emotional reaction. For as President Sukarno said
recently, "For us nationalism is everything. Though nationalism in the West may be an out-of-date doctrine for many,
for us in Asia and Africa it is the mainspring of our efforts."

No doubt oriental and African nationalism is itself of
Western origin, like so much else—like democracy and representative government, engineering and sanitation, newspa-
pers and popular education, broadcasting and atom bombs.
But whereas in Europe nationalism developed gradually out

---

[1] As quoted by G. B. Sansom, *The Western World and Japan* (London,
Cresset Press, Ltd.; New York, Knopf, 1950), p. 289.

of the traditional Western system of small highly-organized political units, who all shared the same culture and the same religious and moral traditions, in Asia and Africa it came into a world of empires and civilizations which had followed their own ways of life for thousands of years and which were for all practical purposes so many distinct and separate worlds. In these different worlds nationalism assumes new forms. In some cases, as in India and China, the nation is identified with the civilization, though the civilization may be larger than the whole of Western Europe; in other cases, as in Africa, the nation may be identified with the tribe, as with the Kikuyu, or else with the inhabitants of a territory which has recently possessed a common administration, though a foreign one. Again, in the Islamic countries nationalism operates on two planes and represents both a common pan-Arab or pan-Islamic unity and territorial units like Syria or Irak.

But everywhere among the great civilizations of the East and the tribal societies of Africa, the new nationalist movement possesses certain common characteristics—it is anti-foreign and, especially, anti-Western and anti-colonial, and it is democratic in the sense that it appeals to the sentiment of the broad mass of the common people and bases itself on the principles of the self-determination of peoples and the rights of man.

In fact, one may say that it is only through the oriental nationalist movement that Western democratic ideas have penetrated the East, and thus oriental nationalism, though apparently anti-European, has in fact been the chief agent of the diffusion of European ideas. No doubt in the nineteenth century liberal-democratic ideas had already begun to affect the oriental world, especially in India and Japan and in the Near East, but they were confined to a small elite and though they made some very distinguished converts, they aroused considerable popular antagonism. It was only in their militant nationalist form that the new ideas gained a wide measure of popular support and became a revolutionary force. But as a revolutionary force they proved even more effective against the old oriental order than against Western Imperialism. It was the nationalists who destroyed the Khalifate, and the Chinese monarchy, which was the most ancient political institution in the world. And this was one of the greatest paradoxes of recent history, since both these institutions had always been regarded as the chief bulwarks of Asiatic resistance to Western influence, and at the very moment when the Turkish nationalists were destroying the Khalifate, the Indian Moslems were organizing a great campaign against the British Empire in its defence.

Consequently oriental nationalism does not mean, as one might suppose, a reaction in defence of traditional oriental culture; on the contrary it means the adoption or appropriation by the Eastern peoples of Western culture. It stands for a new way of life which is as a rule secularist and anti-traditional. The communist states are the most extreme example of this, since they deliberately aim at rebuilding the whole social edifice on the basis of an ideology which originated in London in the Victorian age, and was developed down to the smallest detail in twentieth-century Russia. But the same occidentalizing tendency is to be seen in purely nationalist states which are not in any way contaminated by communist ideology. Thus, the introduction of the new order in Turkey was marked by the systematic secularization of the Turkish state and culture—the abolition of Islam as the state religion, the introduction of a new legal code based on European models and the substitution of the Latin alphabet for the Arabic script.

When one considers the strength of the forces that these movements had to contend with—the organized political and economic power of the European world on the one hand, and the age-long influence of religion and custom and law on the other—their success seems almost miraculous. There were, however, two great factors in their favour. In the first place, the ordinary man had become convinced of the efficacy of Western techniques. He had learnt the lesson in the hard school of war. Even the most conservative, who remained entirely convinced of the superiority of oriental religion and culture, could not shut their eyes to the military and economic power of the West, and at a very early date they recognized that it was necessary to learn the secrets of Western technical efficiency if they were to survive.

To do this they had to accept some degree of Western education. But it proved impossible to limit education to purely technical subjects. Western techniques were inseparable from Western ideas, and the students who were trained in Europe and America or under Western teachers became converts to the Western way of life, and apostles of Western social and political ideas. Thus there grew up all over the East, and at a later period in Africa also, a new educated class which was entirely alienated from the old learned classes—the Confucian scholars in China, the Brahmins in

India and the Ulema in Islam—and which shared the culture of the student class of the West and especially of the liberal and revolutionary intelligentsia.

It was this new class that created the modern nationalist movement in the East. Their indoctrination with Western ideas only made them more determined to assert their equality with the European and to claim the right to national self-determination. As the conservatives had been ready to accept Western aims and Western military methods to defend themselves against the West, so the new nationalist intelligentsia were prepared to accept Western education, Western ideas and the whole apparatus of Western culture in order to shake off their material dependence on the West and to take part on equal terms in the social and intellectual life of the modern world.

Thus oriental nationalism is essentially an educational movement. It had its origin in the student class which had an unbounded faith in the value of Western education, and its progress involves a vast movement of re-education which aims at converting the illiterate peasant masses of Asia into fully conscious citizens of the modern democratic state. It is in this field that the success of the nationalists has been most remarkable. They have not succeeded as yet in modernizing the economy of the Asiatic peoples, nor have they made very marked progress in raising the standard of life of the peasant. But they have made revolutionary changes in the sphere of popular education and in combating illiteracy. Fifty years ago popular education hardly existed in Asia; today it is almost universal, at least in theory. And all this has been accompanied by an awakening of the mind of the masses, which is changing the whole spirit of oriental culture. It is no longer possible to speak of the Unchanging East, for the East is being transformed under our eyes as rapidly as—perhaps even more rapidly than—Europe was changed during the Industrial Revolution.

This is the great achievement of oriental nationalism, and it is not limited to a single class or country, but affects the whole of Asia and is rapidly extending to Africa as well. Hence the paradox that nationalism is an international movement; international not only in its external influence, but also in its social and ideological constitution. While the old cultures of the East were so highly differentiated that they appear as separate worlds, the new nationalist movements are everywhere the same. They have the same kind of leaders drawn from the same student class, which is almost an international one; they are embodied in the same type of political parties, they use the same types of propaganda, and they advocate similar programmes of social reform and the same modern type of universal compulsory education. No doubt this internationalism is superficial, since it is confined to the educated minorities. But since these minorities are the politically active section of the population and since they are constantly increasing owing to the spread of education and the intensification of nationalist propaganda, it would be very unwise to underestimate its importance. Although it is hardly possible to conceive of an United States of Asia, there is a growing sense of international community and a growing desire for closer relations between the Asiatic and African peoples, and the Bandung conference or conferences mark an important step towards the realization of this community.

The force behind this new international community is not unity of culture, since there is no common Asiatic culture, still less a common Afro-Asian one. Neither is it a common political ideology, since it includes both Communist and anti-Communist parties and states. In a sense it is a racialist movement, but it represents no common racial unity; rather is it an anti-racialist movement, which represents the common reaction of all the non-European peoples against the political power, the economic privilege and the racial prejudice of Western Europeans and Americans. This racial element in the nationalist movement is of course greatly intensified by the colour question and the existence of a colour bar in certain countries. It is easy enough to understand this in the United States and the West Indies and South and East Africa, where white men and Negroes are brought into close relations within a single society which is dominated by the white man. At first sight, however, it seems difficult to see what bearing it has on Asiatic nationalism, where the conditions are totally different and where language and religion play a much greater part than complexion in determining men's social status and affiliation, and where the differences of colour within a single state are often greater than those between some Asiatics and some Europeans. Moreover, in Asia the boot is on the other foot, since the Arabs and the high-caste Indian have always been convinced of their racial superiority to the European, while the Chinese have always possessed a sense of cultural superiority which is infinitely stronger than anything that has ever been known in Europe.

The fact remains, however, that the Asiatic has suffered

in the past from the arrogance and bad manners or tactlessness of the European trader and colonist and administrator, and that this experience has made him intensely resentful of all Western claims to superiority and very sympathetic to the Africans and the American Negroes who suffer from social discrimination on purely racial grounds.

There is a danger that the growing internationalism of the East may not make for world peace but may only deepen the breach between East and West, and unite the Asian and African peoples in a common front against the West. We see the first fruits of this movement in the Bandung Conference of 1955, and in the growing tendency of the Arab peoples to look to Russia and China for support against the West.

But how far can this movement go without endangering the independence of the nationalist movements themselves? So long as the West still retains the vestiges of its economic and political power in Asia and Africa, Soviet imperialism and oriental nationalism can co-operate in an anti-colonialist policy. But the moment the West withdraws from the East, the new peoples of the East will find themselves faced with a new imperialism which may prove much more formidable than that which has been displaced. Even at the present time there is a growing contradiction between the ideologies and cultures of the new "people's democracies" of China and the satellite states of the Soviet world, and the medieval theocratic monarchies of Saudi Arabia and the Yemen, which owe their power and importance to the American oil companies; and the success of the present regime in Egypt depends on maintaining a delicate balance between the two.

Above all we must remember that all the new nationalist and Communist parties have their own oppositions to contend with, and these oppositions are more truly nationalist —that is to say more representative of the national traditions of their cultures—than are the dominant parties. Thus, behind the dominant parties, which are modernist, secularist and occidentalist, we find a series of opposition parties which are devoted to the intransigent defence of cultural and religious tradition. In India there is the Mahasabha, the representative of orthodox Hinduism, which was the chief opponent of the Congress Party, as well as a number of Communal national movements like that of the Sikhs. In Pakistan there is the Islamic Party, which utterly rejects the compromise with the secularism which is the official policy of the present regime. In Egypt there is the Muslim Brotherhood, which has been forcibly suppressed by Colonel Nasser's government, and in Indonesia there have been similar movements which have led to civil war.

It is more difficult to speak of such movements in the Communist territories, not merely because they have been ruthlessly repressed, but even more because the whole force of the totalitarian propaganda system is directed to minimizing and misinterpreting them. From the beginning Soviet Communism recognized the importance of the nationalities and did all it could to avoid the mistakes of the Tzarist government, and to win over the national minorities to the Revolution. To this end it established the numerous Constituent National Republics and Autonomous Regions which make up the U.S.S.R., and granted very liberal linguistic and cultural rights to every national group. At the same time the nominal rights of the national republics to complete autonomy and self-determination were contradicted by the strict monopoly of power by the local Communist parties, so that any genuine opposition or any real assertion of nationalist views was stigmatized as counter-revolutionary, reactionary and anti-democratic, and was ruthlessly suppressed. In spite of this there has been no lack of nationalist resistance movements, and whole tribes and peoples have been decimated, deported and even destroyed.

Thus the Soviet policy to nationalism consists of two contradictory elements: on the one hand an ultra-liberal, theoretical attitude to cultural autonomy; on the other, an Assyrian ruthlessness against any assertion of ideological or political independence. But these two elements are not so contradictory as they appear at first sight. For the larger the number of national minority groups that are officially recognized, the greater is the disproportion between each of them and the vast monolithic unity of the Great Russian people and of the Russian Soviet Republic which embraces seventy-seven per cent or more of the total territory. As against this great unity of a hundred million Russians, Soviet ethnologists recognize the existence of one hundred and sixty-eight other nationalities in the Union. Most of these are Asiatic nationalities, but even the most important of them, like the Uzbeks or the Kazaks, only number between three and five million apiece. Yet for all that the Turkish peoples of Central Asia possess a very strong sense of common racial and historical tradition, which under more favourable circumstances might well have created a nation. This finds literary expression in the work of the Kazak poet, Maghjan Jumbay of Yedisu, for though he took a leading part in the long war of resistance of the Kazaks against the Soviets, he is not so much concerned with the practical issue of Kazak political freedom, as with the cause of the Turkish peoples in general. He writes of

The sacred Issik Kol, on which the first Turk
Born of the grey wolf, saw the light of the world.
The two rivers, Jaihun and Saihun
And between them the sacred graves of the ancestors.
The great mountains of Turan, Khan Tengri reaching to
heaven;
Look now to the mountains and think how the Turks suffer
in bondage.[2]

And it is remarkable that though the movement of resistance to Russia in Central Asia was mainly inspired by strict Islamic orthodoxy, like some of the other opposition movements and parties I have discussed, the poet himself looks for something different—some new religious leader who will bring salvation to the Turks:

Thou gavest to every land,
To the poor Arabia, nurse of camels,
A prophet to show the way and a holy book,
But to us Turks this grace has not been given,
We have followed prophets from divers lands
And set our faith in holy words,
But the way has not been shown us.
Lord, send us a prophet to show us that way.[3]

This Messianic appeal is not a mere literary device on the

[2] Translated by O. K. Caroe, *The Soviet Empire* (London, Macmillan; New York, St. Martin's Press, 1953), p. 227.
[3] *Ibid.*, p. 228.

part of a modern nationalist man of letters. For already a generation before the poet appealed to the Turks of Anatolia to go back in spirit to the Altai and "mount the golden throne of their forefathers," the primitive pagan Turks of the Altai had actually produced a prophet who announced the imminent return to earth of the last descendant of Chinghiz Khan, who would deliver the Turks from Russian oppression and unite them in a new kingdom. It was called the religion of the White Burkhan and was quickly repressed by the Russians. But it is extremely doubtful whether Maghjan Jumbay had ever heard of it.

Similar movements are to be found all over the world. They were especially strong in North America during the eighteenth and nineteenth centuries and are represented today in the so-called Cargo cults of New Guinea. But they are not confined to primitive peoples, for the great T'ai P'ing movement which convulsed China in the nineteenth century, and almost led to the downfall of the Empire, belonged to the same class of movement.

Now, at first sight there seems little in common between these Messianic social movements, which the ethnologists term nativistic, and the nationalisms which I discussed in the first part of this essay. For the latter are secular and political and modernist, while the former are reactionary and religious and irrational. They look back to an imaginary golden age of native culture, while the latter look forward to a social Utopia in the future. Yet the difference is not as great as it seems. Every revolutionary movement has a Messianic element. Communism itself is a secular Messianism, which announces the judgment of the Capitalist world and the coming of a new order of social justice. The nativistic movements are more religious and less political than the nationalist ones, because they answer to the situation of peoples who have no opportunity of political action and who are faced with an alien culture which is overwhelmingly strong, as was the case with the Indians of the Plains in the nineteenth century. At the present time, however, we are witnessing the appearance of new movements like the Mau Mau movement in Kenya, which are intermediate between the two types—which are at once nationalist and nativistic, and which combine a political programme with an appeal to irrational motives and forces.

And we may ask whether such a combination of elements is not to be seen nearer home in such movements as National Socialism in Germany, which has made a more violent impact on the world than any of the more orthodox forms of political nationalism.

The defeat of Hitlerism does not mean that we have seen the last of such movements. In our modern democratic world irrational forces lie very near the surface, and their sudden eruption under the impulse of nationalist or revolutionary ideologies is the greatest of all the dangers that threaten the modern world. The fact that oriental nationalism has awakened the world and torn it loose from its old moorings in tradition and custom does not necessarily make for peace. On the contrary, it makes it more inflammable and more exposed to the influence of sudden irrational mass movements.

It is at this point that the need for a reassertion of Christian principles becomes evident. Nationalism is essentially a force of division. It contains no universal principle of unity or international order. If the world is left to the unrestricted development of nationalistic movements, it will become a Babel of people who not only speak different tongues, but follow different laws and seek divergent ends. As a means of evoking common loyalty and common action within a single society, there is no denying the value and efficiency of nationalism. But as an ultimate principle of human action, it is morally inadequate and socially destructive. Left to itself, it becomes a form of mass egotism and self-idolatry which is the enemy of God and man. This has always been realized in some degree by the great civilizations of the past. All of them have admitted the existence of a higher law above that of the tribe and the nation, and consequently subordinated national interest and political power to the higher spiritual values which are derived from this source. On this point there is a consensus of principle which unites all the world religions and all the great civilizations of the past alike in the East and the West. All agree that the social order does not exist merely to serve men's interests and passions. It is the expression of a sacred order by which human action is conformed to the order of heaven and the eternal law of divine justice.

Now, in so far as nationalism denies this principle and sets up the nation and the national State as the final object of man's allegiance, it represents the most retrograde movement that the world has ever seen, since it means a denial of the great central truth on which civilization was founded, and a return to the pagan idolatries of tribal barbarism.

We cannot ignore the serious nature of this challenge, for